GOODBYE LAKE TAHOE
GOODBYE INDIAN JOE

Buck Custer (signature)

A NOVEL BY

BUCK CUSTER

Wasteland Press
Shelbyville, KY USA
www.wastelandpress.net

Goodbye Lake Tahoe, Goodbye Indian Joe
by Buck Custer

First Printing – July 2008
ISBN: 978-1-60047-230-5

Printed in the U.S.A.

PART I: JEFF

Chapter One

He moved slowly thru the tall pines, almost silently but for the occasional crackling of the needles underfoot, dropping down from the deeper shaded area above, to pick his way thru the underbrush of manzanita and sage, then crossing a little more quickly through the light splotched thinner stand. At the edge of the meadow, he stopped, a tall man, sunbrowned in faded green khaki, motionless and watching. In front of him and partway out in the meadow, a lone dead cedar stood resignedly, its whitened bark a silent, if striking, testimony to many winters there. But crouching and so still he seemed a part of the ageless rocks, trees and sand, himself, he gazed beyond, down across the vast yellowing field to the great blue Lake where he had been a boy.

Behind him a brook burbled along, springing from some underground source further up; while in the trees, mountain jays hopped, then flew, then hopped again, flashing blue fire thru sunny patches. There was in the early morning sunshine almost the old feeling, he thought—the forever timelessness of before—so that for the barest of instants, he expected the doe and fawn he once had seen there to emerge thru the alders and drink cautiously from the stream.

Once it had been the most wonderful place he would ever see, though perhaps he hadn't fully realized it then, certainly not as deeply as now in his anguish.

This was Glenbrook, the historic heart of Lake Tahoe, where John Fremont had camped, and Mark Twain; and where Presidents had visited. But even more, it was where he'd grown up—in whose forests and streams and lakeshore he was so deeply rooted.

Somehow it had never occurred to him that it could happen here. Never once while he was away had it even crossed his mind. And yet the truth was that it had happened, in spite of anything he'd thought or hadn't thought; and, as it was his own place in a personal way, there was somewhere in his groping perhaps even an affrontedness and a non-comprehension at his not having been consulted.

True, the reared up condominiums on the other side of the meadow were ungainly aberrations, garish light pink and gray and arranged in courts or semi-circles. Close together and seeming more like barracks than apartments, with a sort of built in shabbiness made more apparent by the grandeur of the surroundings. With paved streets gashing the slope, connecting one ugly section to another, and complete with little road signs and pointing arrows. And other signs even more colorful, proclaiming square footage, terms and how many bedrooms to the unit. And yet—and yet not so different from a thousand other developments that had scarred the countryside before.

Still in his mind's eye, he saw it as it had been and always should be. His throat constricted and a choking sob nearly escaped him, stifled immediately, however, by a deliberate screwing down of his bitterness—an effort resulting at once in a tight squeezing across his chest. He wanted to cry out even, but then knew there was no one to hear, nor anyone who could feel or understand it as he did. He thought that he was at last face to face with a kind of final hopelessness, so that for a fleeting, lucid moment he even wondered about going on with his plan. But then this, too, was at once overwhelmed by the pure flame fierceness of his bitterness.

He straightened up, his temples throbbing, then strangely felt himself to be near orgasm. He breathed deeply to gain control, one hand gripping the thin young sapling beside him; then marshaling his forces, brought within himself a terrible focusing of his brain—so that the resolve that followed was of stone. For many days and nights thereafter, he made the long trek down from the ridge, thru the quiet forest to the same spot—each time with heavy pack loaded across his shoulders, the contents of which (electrical wire, detcord and plastic explosives) he cached carefully in the rocks. Then with field glasses, and sometimes with pad and pencil,

4

he'd watch, sketch and make his calculations. When finally he'd assembled all that was necessary, and when he knew the hours of the workmen who were doing the finish work, and the habits of the watchman at the ornamented gate, be began.

Night after night, he stole thru the tall meadow grass, packing along as much explosive as he could manage; and in the dead small hours between two and five AM, when the watchman habitually dozed in the gate-keeping station, expertly and methodically packed the C-4 *plastique* in the crawl spaces, around those gas lines where the gas was connected, and on load bearing walls where it was not. He used a knot he'd learned in Vietnam—which itself served as a detonator and made the use of a blasting cap unnecessary—to tie the detcord (or exploding fuse) to the C-4, then afterwards simply left the attached detcord coiled up and ready in the crawl spaces.

On the final evening, needing the cover of darkness for his getaway, he slipped in early, reaching the buildings at eight, just after dark and after the guard had checked routinely for locked doors. He worried about the guard's wakefulness and, entering the crawl spaces, allowed himself but one blink of the tiny pen light he was carrying, just enough to locate the ends of the coiled detcord, which in each case he pulled along with him back outside. Then feeling himself naked despite the still un-removed brush in the clearing between the buildings, struggled to stay low to the ground and still work quickly.

He attached each end of the detcord he'd brought out to a main stem center point, using also in this case two blasting caps which he taped in lengthwise—pencil wide, metal and highly explosive. And with his heart pounding with fear and anticipation, he had on several occasions to stop and tell himself to 'get calm,' not pleased by the shaking in his hands.

Then he would wait and, raising his head slightly, watch the booth, which was about a quarter of a mile distant and whose fluorescent illumination was all the light visible, but for the stars. He watched, and at one point the guard stood up, his blue uniform plainly visible in spite of the distance; so that he caught his breath, thinking somehow the man had sensed his presence and was

5

coming outside. However, he did not, but rather just stretched, walked around in a couple of tight circles and then sat back down.

And after that, all that remained was to stretch a piece of electrical wire from the two caps to the little spark generator, or "blasting machine," he'd left hidden another fifty feet away in the brush. It was a small and insignificant-seeming object in the darkness, weighing barely a pound and able to fit in the palm of his hand. He paused then to consider all that he had done, crouched in the manzanita and sage with the scents mingled and strong in his nostrils, forcing himself to remember one last time, also, what had been, and what had come to be. There in the pitch darkness, he saw vividly again the golden meadow, blue lake and verdant forest, all glistening as before in the early morning dew.

Then with the certainty that no workmen were there, and that the watchman was once again sleeping in his booth, he turned suddenly and, with a fierce grunt of something like satisfaction, cranked hard on the handle and blew the new "Tahoe Paradise" into a huge ascending fireball in the midnight sky.

Chapter Two

Gambling profits are the principal support of big-time racketeering and gangsterism. These profits provide the financial resources whereby ordinary criminals are converted into big-time racketeers, political bosses, pseudo businessmen, and alleged philanthropists . . . .

The legalization of gambling would not terminate the widespread predatory activities of criminal gangs and syndicates. The history of legalized gambling in Nevada and in other parts of the country gives no assurance that mobsters and racketeers can be converted into responsible businessmen through the simple process of obtaining state and local license for their gambling enterprises.[1]

He moved swiftly then, replacing the triggering device in his pack, shouldering the pack and then crossing the upper corner of the meadow to the creek. In the glow of the mounting flames, shadows flickered eerily, leaping out alarmingly across the meadow towards him. Still unflinchingly, he headed downstream, eschewing the easier, beckoning route to the East. Would-be pursuers would expect him to go upstream—to get as far away as fast as possible—and for that reason he would not. He stepped into

---

[1] U.S. Senate, Third Interim Report of the Special Committee to Investigate Crime in Interstate Commerce, Report No. 307, 82nd Congress. P.2.

the icy coldness of the dark water, gasping involuntarily as it covered him to the waist; then crouching low so that his head was always beneath the bordering grass and willows, moved crablike, stealthily and carefully over the algae-slickened rocks two hundred yards downstream to the Lake.

The watchman had called others by now, he knew, fire trucks were on the way, and already lights were coming on in scattered summer cabins. Still, the focus was on the fire and not the cause, and would continue that way for awhile, as long as he didn't allow himself to be seen.

Had he elected to go upstream, he would be already further away and safer for the time being at least. But once they had determined it was sabotage—and it would be obvious soon enough—and once they had failed to catch him at one of their roadblocks, or out on the Lake with their boat patrols, the next logical place to look would be up the stream. If one followed the creek in that direction far enough, eventually he'd hit old abandoned Highway 50 and would have his own private thoroughfare thru the forest and up the canyon—easy walking and running until reaching the new highway which led right out of the basin. It would have been easy, but too easy, he knew, and too obvious; and now his very survival depended on not doing the obvious.

He stuck to the creek bed, grasping at the willows and pulling himself along, keenly aware of every passing minute and of every sloshing sound he was making—wanting desperately to strike out and run—reaching finally the edge of the beach after a good twenty minutes of agonized slogging. Still even then remaining deliberate, pausing while still in the willows to check the zipper on his pack—flat, waterproofed and up on his back. Then afterwards, peering out at the beach for another several minutes. Here, the flickering light from the flames was more diffused by distance, so that shapes were more obscure. Still, when he stepped out, satisfied that no one was there, he could feel the fire's heat at his back and was surprised at its intensity. Wraith-like, he crossed the sand and entered the water, moving so lightly and quickly that an observer—had there been one—might have wondered whether he'd seen anyone at all.

He gritted his teeth against the cold and ducked immediately under, swimming rapidly though soundlessly and parallel to the shore, reaching finally the old wooden pier which stretched far out into the lake—warmed now from the exertion, and glancing but for the briefest instant in towards the shore.

Still the vision etched itself with shocking clarity upon his troubled mind. Flames shot up in the night sky behind the old inn, illuminating it so that even the veranda fronting the dock was visible, as well as the two tall, hundred year old poplar trees which had framed the entrance always, and stood, as sentinels against a changing world. And he knew if a strong wind didn't come up soon out of the West, the inn would be burned, too; and for that he felt a stabbing pang of regret.

Yes, the developers had slated it for takeover and conversion to a gambling casino; still they hadn't yet, and every day of its existence could be counted as a blessing. Termination point for the great log rafts of the past century, lodging for Ulysses Grant when he'd been the President and for numerous others—peaceful, sedate, historic—doomed now by one of those who'd loved her most.

He choked on the water, stifling a wracking cough, then set his mind again and swam under the old wooden pier for the last time—remembering, nevertheless, echoing sounds from his youth: boots on planks and a boat squeaking against an old rubber tire. Again he lingered for the barest instant, then was out the other side and away—without having to face ever the day of demolition and the all new plastic and metal marina that would surely follow.

Now a hundred and fifty feet from shore, he swam still soundlessly, on the surface and breast-stroking powerfully, purposely to the North and towards the mouth of a second stream. When he was planning, he had thought for awhile to swim the lake—across the eleven miles to the other side—confident even of his ability to do so and of his strength to endure the cold. They would never expect anyone to do it, he knew, and in that way it was appealing. Still there was the problem of timing. In the morning as he was nearing the other shore, it would be light and there would be boat traffic; and should someone notice him swimming a mile or two from shore, he necessarily would be regarded as other than a casual swimmer. Late season tourists on that shore would increase his chances of being detected geometrically, also; and then too, assuming he did make it in undetected, he would be spent from the swim with nothing in reserve if a burst of energy were needed.

He swam on, further out from shore now where a sweeping beam from a flashlight wouldn't pick him up, passing old pilings left from a hundred years before, when there were sawmills at Glenbrook and the virgin timbers were ferried there in rafts from the Lake's south end. And then in the dim distance, he could make out the clump of alders marking the other creek.

At once, he was seized with the sudden urge to abandon the breaststroke, to change to an all out crawl and be done with it— feeling his impatience and anxiety rising again and wanting to be in the creek bed and working finally away to the East. He even brought one arm up and over, only to be reminded of the awkwardness of the backpack; then heard, or perhaps felt, the vibration of an outboard motor.

Stunned, he stopped swimming, his heart pounding furiously. He looked around desperately to locate the boat in the darkness, then sculled laterally, carefully to the shadow of one lone old piling, still unable to see and trying to control his breathing as the sound came ever closer.

'Who was it?' he thought, 'And what were they doing out at this hour? Surely, they couldn't be on to him so soon.' It was after all the middle of the night, too late for evening cruising and too early for fishing. Still they came on, whoever they were, not moving rapidly, showing no running lights, and with voices muffled over the drone of the engine.

When he finally made them out—dark on dark, coming from the West—they seemed headed directly for the piling. And then it occurred to him that they might just be coming to investigate the glow of the fire which reddened the sky behind him. He watched from behind the piling, taking controlled deep breaths as the shape grew less obscure. Then in what seemed the last possible moment, he gripped the knotty, slippery piling and pulled himself all the way under, wrapping his legs around as well.

He heard the rising buzz of the propeller coming ever closer under the water, unnervingly; and, praying that he hadn't miscalculated and gone under too soon, he held himself there with a grim outpouring of his strength and will. The buzz sounded louder still, rising incessantly, irritatingly, so that he could feel it in his teeth; then staying at that level for a heart-stopping moment before finally, imperceptibly at first, starting to recede.

His chest felt as if it would burst, and his head; and still he stayed down waiting, waiting, forcing his body around to the other side of the pile from the direction he was sure the boat had headed. Then, only when he thought he might pass out, did he allow himself to ease his face up thru the surface into the welcoming world of night-time air, stifling his gasp with an even greater force of will.

He could still hear the boat, but no longer the muffled voices; yet he waited determinedly, patiently some more, knowing those in the boat would be seeing the flames more clearly now and would go either directly in, or perhaps turn away, depending upon what business they had there. Neither of which concerned him particularly at that point, as long as they didn't come back in the direction from which they'd come. He waited, then knew at length he'd escaped detection, and that was all.

The boat was lost from view and didn't return; and he began to swim again, realizing once more that discovery in the small concentrated area could prove only fatal. A search concentrated at Glenbrook and in Glenbrook waters with the law knowing he was in their midst would be a sure and deadly tightening noose; whereas without detection, the assumption would be that the bomber or terrorist had escaped naturally, rapidly by car or boat—so that necessarily the search and the searchers would be immediately fanned out.

He swam again in grim awareness of time passing, and of his own planned time table, the darker line of the shore still distant across the water's expanse. In his impatience, he even supposed a current working against him and that he might never reach the alders guarding the creek's mouth. At last though, he did glide into the shallows, then moved again crablike thru the rocks and up into the cover of the trees.

He was cold and dripping, but immediately found the staff he'd cut and left in the brush the night before. Then he was moving upstream, still in the creek, feeling for footholds in the slippery rocks as before, groping along thru the darkness, not fast but steadily, and always with control.

A hundred years before, a settler family had operated a little, narrow gage railroad between Glenbrook and Spooners Summit, just a few miles to the East. The train was used for hauling big logs up to a giant V-shaped flume trough, which in turn ran for twelve miles down to the Carson Valley. From there the logs were dragged by mules up to Virginia City and the Comstock—to be used as shoring in the mines, which honey-combed the mountains there to unimaginable depths, numbering in the thousands of feet. Vast quantities of timber were necessary for the crib-like structures forming the shafts, so that eventually there were no trees left on the Eastern side at all. Then finally, the mountains around Tahoe were even de-nuded as well.

The old railbed was still there, winding up from the lake, though generally following the creek for the first several miles, before twisting sharply in several torturous, altitude-gaining switchbacks. And, having learned the area as a boy, and having re-scouted it carefully again over the past several weeks, he struggled along in the streambed for a good forty-five minutes, trying to avoid sloshing noises while wrestling with willows and alders which in places virtually choked the stream—careful, ever careful not to break, bend or leave sign, until reaching finally a great boulder patch which made the stream impassable.

A late pale moon offered scant illumination, but even that was more that he would have liked. Still, he paused for several moments, standing in the shadow of a tall pine, listening and watching; then sat shiveringly on an already wet rock at the stream's edge. If searchers had gotten wind of him somehow and came along soon, he wanted them to find *no sign*, thus he not only avoided wetting dry rocks, but paused now to zip open the carefully conceived pack. Inside were dry pants, shirt and a towel, as well as a pair of soft, dry moccasins. And drying and changing hurriedly, he wrung out his wet shorts in the creek to cut down on weight, and replaced them in the pack along with what was left of his torn wet sneakers and all important water proofed canister of matches. Then afterwards, he struck the old roadbed running.

He would follow it for only a couple of miles, to the point where the switchbacks started, then would head off thru the forest, opting in this case for the faster, more direct route. It was over four miles along the old railroad bed to Spooner's Pond and the logging road that led from there to Marlette Lake, but only three miles direct. And with his adrenalin flowing as now, the added steepness was scarcely a consideration. He flew uphill, finally releasing the frustration pent up by the agonizingly slow progress in the creeks, and the also necessarily slow swim—glad to run now and to feel at last he was truly getting away.

Soft moonlight dappled the forest floor and the hundred year old roadbed, but the dry moccasins left little trace on the firm packed ground, not indicating more than the path of any chance hiker. He ran strongly up the gradually climbing incline, smelling the pines and feeling the strength in his chest, mindful however of the danger of a turned ankle and searching consciously the dimness for depression and unevenness. A dozen minutes farther on, he stopped momentarily where a trail from the South intersected the roadbed and where, just beyond the trail, the creek, bending around from the North, ducked thru a metal culvert. He leaned forward with hands on his knees, breathing deeply and trying to look in every direction at once, able finally to hold his breath and listen. Then hearing nothing but a mournful, distant owl, started off again, still headed North but walking for awhile now and needing still to catch his breath. He thought he'd probably run too hard in the beginning; still a little farther on, the roadbed turned back abruptly South at the start of the first switchback, and then he was away from it, striking off thru the forest where he couldn't run much anyway.

Here the floor was thick with deep beds of slippery needles and, while he knew it would be slower here, he felt encouraged to be this far along. He headed East and a little South then, crossing the old railbed two more times, where the old log trains had wound their way up the steep grade. Then after another hour of carefully checking his direction thru the trees, he emerged momentarily to cross the empty highway and dropped down the old dirt road to the reservoir at Spooner's.

Now after the silence of the forest, his moccasins crunched noticeably on the sandy ground and, with the first light streaks of dawn showing over the eastern range, he knew that soon, inevitably, he would see other people and they would see him. He drifted down off the old road into some heavy brush just up from the pond and, in the dim early light, surveyed the surroundings cautiously. Somewhere out on the water, or more probably in the bordering marsh grass, a duck quacked and, listening intently, he thought he heard a buck snort, too, though he couldn't be sure.

Otherwise though, there was nothing and, satisfied at last, he eased himself down on his haunches, anxious for the light now when a solitary hiker would be commonplace and scarcely noticeable. Now for an hour, he thought, he'd stay out of sight, eat, rest a bit, and then head up the old logging road to the North. Marlette Lake was up there, just another five miles, and also the great Senator's summer camp retreat; and at the thought of the latter, he grunted and allowed himself a thin smile.

"How I'd like . . . ," he thought, but knew it was impossible now and just as quickly put it from his mind.

He took a plastic bag from the pack which he'd set down on a rock and, taking some jerky from it, chewed hungrily. He didn't like the taste, nor the laboriousness of it, but he was weary now and needed the strength. He was twenty-four and wiry tough; but 'swimming and running all night would tire any man,' he thought sardonically, allowing himself suddenly, unexpectedly another faint grin. 'I bet they're fit to be tied by now,' he thought, 'even the Senator.'

He lay back against the pack, allowing his legs the luxury of a stretch, feeling immediately his whole body begin to relax. He knew it was dangerous, but in his fatigue there was a kind of lightheaded euphoria, and he very nearly lost his perspective. He breathed deeply for a time and wanted nothing in the world as much as to lie all the way down and sleep. He thought probably no one would see him there if he slept all morning; and, even if they did, what would it prove anyway? He felt himself drifting off, but then at once, fortuitously, heard voices and was immediately alert.

Up on his haunches, one hand gripping the pack strap and with his heart in his throat, he listened as they came down the trail from the campground to the North. At first just a murmur, the voices grew rapidly louder and then, as he heard laughter, also, he felt himself relax. Pursuers would be silent in their stalking he knew, and decidedly non-jocular, so that he decided they must be fishermen who would head directly for the pond.

Still, he remained crouching and scarcely breathing, hearing the crunching of their footsteps drawing ever nearer—wishing he'd pulled back a little further into the brush and further from the old road. It was too late now, though, and for a moment the doubt assailed his mind—that he was about to be discovered and wouldn't know what to do.

But then they were past, the sounds of their footsteps diminishing; and afterwards he sidled away crablike, dragging the pack with him deeper into the brush before getting back up to his feet. Then he swung the pack again across his shoulders and moved off prematurely—knowing for appearance sake that additional light was desirable, but now, after the fishermen, unable to tolerate any more stillness.

Moving quickly and stealthily for the next half hour, staying still deep in the brush and avoiding the trail until the increasing light was more favorable—until the sun lifted up over the eastern range and bathed the world in a soft orange glow. At which point he intersected the old dirt logging road that led to Marlette, heaving a little sigh as he left the cover of the brush and struck the road wearing the different hat of a vacationing hiker.

Chapter Three

Jeff Hamil was in Viet Nam for two and a half years, one of an elite group of demolition experts that mined enemy harbors, blew up bridges behind the lines—sometimes singlehandedly—and disarmed enemy bombs that no one else would get near. Thanks in large part to what Indian Joe had taught him, he survived, though he thought Joe might have had mixed feelings even about that.

He came back to the States in the end—to the University in Reno—and enrolled in a literature class, thinking only to lay back for awhile, read and forget. But then the students were still strident and puffed up with the perceived "successes" of their war protests; and, though he suffered them stoically, numbly, when spring came, he desperately needed someone to be near.

Her name was Sue Marie and he met her in a First Aid class where he was assisting the instructor. He noticed her when she got sick to her stomach in the midst of a gory and realistic traffic film. Steadfastly claiming it was due to something she'd eaten; though, seeing her vulnerable, he preferred to think otherwise.

She was a student assistant in the library—a senior of medium height, with dark hair and eyes, and a kind of Western outdoor beauty, reflecting freshness and, in some way perhaps, the skiing and mountain hiking that she loved. She had about her also, though, a remarkable soberness; and undoubtedly that was what attracted Jeff Hamil first, along with a quiet and very low voice which set her further apart. Unfortunately however, in his need to unburden, he missed something else, which was critical and should have been easily detectable—a certain sort of twinkle in her brown eyes which at least partially belied the serious bearing—giving promise in fact of a playful side that needed especially to laugh. But then too, Jeff Hamil had never had much success or experience with the ladies before the war—had never really had a steady girl friend—and the Vietnamese bar girls he'd had, he'd known only in desperation.

He and Sue Marie had gone on small dates at first, walks to the Student Union for coffee, then later for pizza and movies; and he could tell she liked him, giving him warm, melting looks of greeting that surprised him. No one had ever looked at him quite like that, and once he'd even turned around and glanced behind, thinking it must have been directed at someone else. He brought her flowers and little gifts continually then—gestures which she nevertheless seemed to treat strangely indifferently, taking them for granted in a way which faintly bothered him, and which belied the warm, melting looks. Still in his lonesomeness, he needed her too much, and very suddenly was in love with her, wanting her to share in everything.

He told her very little of the war, though, of the bridges and the bombings; the dead and dying children; and the suffering— having resolved to put those behind. But what he talked of was the country around them, of what it had been, and what had been done to it. This, after all, after everything else, was still his passion, somehow meaning even more now than before. And yet, he felt himself to be alone in a vacuum with no one left who could understand. Ned, his father was gone—died while he was away, the telegram reaching him in the field ten days after the funeral. And Joe was locked up, and Tony in Alaska. So, he was soon dependent on this sober young girl, who at first listened to him, it seemed, with such undivided attention. She drew it all from him, just by being there and listening; and increasingly, when they were apart, he was lost and could scarcely stand it.

Still, in her life there were other influences, not the least of which were the gale force winds of the feminist movement—and voices telling her that love need be skipped altogether, if it meant a dividing of one's self. So that in her youthfulness— impressionable—she was swayed; then despite her soberness, realized too late his dependence.

She grew flip in the face of the continued intensity, being practical after all about living life as it was. 'Why did he care so much about how Lake Tahoe used to be, anyway? It was super now as far as she was concerned, better than anything they had had back in Ohio where she'd been a child!'

In some agony he'd try to explain it, but then increasingly she would seem bored. 'Weren't there any positives in this world?' she wanted to know. 'Where were the good times and when would they begin?'

He drove her to Lake Tahoe for dinner in a car he'd borrowed from an aunt, wanting to take her to Glenbrook to show her what it had been like—where the old inn was where President Grant had eaten; where the ancient steamers had been built; and where forest met meadow and meadow met lake—where, at least when he was a boy, the wild deer drank in numbers from the fresh, clear streams.

She was distant when he picked her up at her parent's home, though lovely, he thought, in gray skirt and crisp, pastel plaid blouse. But glancing sideways at her in the car, he noticed a tightening of her jaw, as she looked ahead. Then felt the first beginning of fear knotting his stomach at the thought she was beginning to slip away.

He tried not to speak anymore for awhile about how it had been before, and about what he believed, and what should have been done. But, it was difficult to exhibit joy, when underneath he felt the way he did. Thus, what conversation they had on the way up to the Lake seemed forced to him and stilted. He could not say with excitement in his voice that, 'yes, they were going to wonderful Lake Tahoe to have a wonderful time,' because he didn't believe it was wonderful anymore, and mostly he was concerned with the hope that at least Glenbrook would be as it had been.

He asked her about her day in the library, and about a test she'd had in a history class, and about her plan to give her old car to her brother. But all the time, it felt false because that wasn't where his head was, and no doubt she knew it. In return, she told him about a rock climbing class she'd signed up for at the Rec Center and—with a blush and uncharacteristic giggle—about the instructor promising her a "personalized" lesson.

Then after crossing the summit and stopping the car on an overlook, it hit him, and for a moment he couldn't even breathe. "The new condominiums" assaulted his senses, his sacred memories and even what was left of hopes and dreams—pink and elephantine in appearance, starting at the water's edge and blanketing the meadows of his childhood, all the way up to the forest—an aberration of such horror that he was overpowered. Out of the car, he actually retched, and retched again, then rested his head on his arms atop the car for what seemed a long time, and while she sat rigid still in her seat.

"Are you all right?" she asked finally when he got back in the car, but there was in her voice a kind of icy contempt for such weakness—for perceived theatrics, anyway—which, in spite of his great upset, was not lost on him.

He didn't say anything, though, but turned the car around and drove back up onto the highway.

"I thought you wanted to eat at the old inn," she said, her voice now disappointed and a little desperate.

But, he couldn't answer her and drove back down the mountain to take her home.

Jeff Hamil followed the old logging road high into the Sierra, the hot early morning sun drawing rivulets of sweat as he climbed steadily thru his fatigue. It was five miles from Spooners to Marlette Lake and a couple more to the isolated reservoir called Hobart. And while he was aware of the distance when he'd first struck the road, to buoy himself he'd tried to forget about the other part—about the steepness which would drain from him the last of his remaining strength.

"Just five more miles and a little bit," he kept saying to himself. "Just five miles and a bit!"

He'd been on the road for only an hour when he was startled by the first hiker, coming on him suddenly face to face around a bend. He was dressed in green shorts and a white T-shirt, and had pack and bedroll strapped across his shoulders—stocky and fortyish with dark, unshaven stubble and beady, black eyes.

"Cold up at Marlette?" Hamil heard his own voice asking pleasantly, while his heart pounded in his chest.

"Last night," was the grunted, not so friendly reply.

So that Hamil merely nodded and went on, climbing without looking back, wondering in spite of himself if the hiker were a cop—if he'd noticed anything about Hamil, his moccasins or long pants. With an effort he shook the thought from his mind, knowing the harm in such imaginings. Once someone had told him if a person said things often enough, they would come to pass and, while he didn't believe it entirely, he knew there was often a correlation between positive thought and positive action—so that he held strongly to the optimism that he wouldn't be found.

Awhile later he met another hiker, a thin, nervous-looking young man, also in shorts and T-shirt, carrying a bedroll, bespectacled and tanned under a lettered red baseball cap announcing that "you only go around once". And Hamil, easier now, spoke to him with something passing for a smile.

"Nice day," he said. To which the other replied at the point of passing, "Super!"

Off to the left in the trees was a Forestry Service shelter, a little tin roofed log hut used primarily by cross country skiers in the winter, but now lying open and empty; and, with the heaviness in his legs warning that there'd soon be cramps, he decided reluctantly on a stop. He crossed the quiet clearing in front, the blue jays scolding and hopping from branch to branch in the tall old pines; then paused beside a wood pile just outside the door, watchful and careful.

But, there was nothing, just a lazy sun-filled summer morning—no movement but for the jays, and the only other sound the timeless buzzing of flies from inside the shelter itself.

He pushed thru the door to find a barrel-shaped, black woodstove and rough hewn table and benches, the interior illuminated from a small window with shutter removed which looked out on the clearing and trail. He slung the pack off onto the table, then collapsed gratefully on one of the benches, arranging himself to see out. He leaned his head back against the wall and put his feet up, staring blankly at the clever and not so clever graffiti carved into the wall and table; then allowed himself to doze, with all that had happened seeming very far away.

A pine cone clattering down on the tin roof jarred him awake, though, and he came to his feet in a single gliding step, looking about wildly. 'What was it? Had somebody come?'

He moved quickly to the door, peering past the jam to the outside, but there was nothing. Then when another cone hit the roof and rolled down a moment later, he had his answer.

Afterwards, he climbed on thru a variety of terrain, from thick pine forest to meadows to thickets, and then to forest once more, not stopping again except to drink at bubbling seeps and crystal rushing creeks—driven by the need for it to be done. Nor was he as careful as he had been, spending much less energy in surveying ahead, delirious with his fatigue, but something more. The earlier communing with the hikers, limited though it was, and then the nap in the public place with no untoward consequences had altered him slightly, subtly removing him from what had gone before. So that now, it was in his own tired mind as if he *were* the hiker he purported to be. When he remembered the other, since it had gone on at night and since it seemed a very long time ago, he could more easily believe it a dream than a reality.

He trudged slowly across a flat, brown meadow, paying little heed to the ancient remains of one of the old flumes which had so interested him in the past—built in Abraham Lincoln's day to skid the virgin timbers down the mountains to the log pond in Carson. He pressed on doggedly—up a last grade before viewing Marlette Lake—fighting off the debilitating knowledge that even at the top he couldn't rest.

Then the small lake opened out below him, deep blue and ruffled in the afternoon sun, the view serving only to turn him away immediately to the East. He had no desire to meet with the great Senator's security forces, whom he was certain had been alerted by now. So, he gave the lake a wide berth, knowing the famed camp spot to be at the opposite end, but taking no chances, striking off laterally thru the trees and moving faster with a real or imagined sense of urgency. Here too, there was a flattening of the terrain that offered relief to his lungs and made it possible to go faster; and then after fifteen minutes of forest, an intersection with the faint trail leading off East. Where, feeling himself relax, he knew it was now less than two miles to the Indian cave.

He staggered at times and his mind wandered, at one point finding himself meandering dazedly down along a stream. But he forced himself to think of the girl again, then with gritted teeth was able to gather himself anew. Then finally, about four o'clock, and after one last gut wrenching ascent, looked down thru gaps in the tall pines on the dam.

There, anciently, the earth had been packed high across the head of a narrow V-shaped canyon, thus backing up Hobart Creek and creating a reservoir of the same name. The level of the lake was maintained by a water master from across the mountains who only rarely jeeped and hiked over to check and, if necessary, adjust the gates; and because it was back in so far, fishermen declined as well.

Still he came down on it cautiously, renewed by the successful arrival, and with an attendant sharpening of his senses. He skirted the marshy south end where the creek flowed in, then made his way stealthily thru the pines along the East side, pausing often to listen and watch. However, there was no one about, and the only sounds were the low, contented quackings of a pair of mallards in the tall grass opposite, and the occasional flippings of trout taking insects at the surface.

He moved on, to the far end, then eased the pack off and allowed himself to sit, resting with his back to a large old cedar— able to see most of the lake, but not visible himself, and unwilling to risk a crossing of the dam till after dark. A chance observer, higher up on the mountain, might spot him there and think it odd; and while he knew the probabilities were remote, still he wanted no complication.

He sat and watched and dozed, then woke suddenly with a start, the coolness of oncoming night penetrating his fatigue. Now in the twilight, he could still make out the dam and, easing himself to his feet, he stretched his weary muscles carefully, then shouldered the pack a last time and filtered out of the trees— keeping a low profile down along the outer face of packed earth to the other side of the dam. Then in the darkness of the trees again, he struck the old trail and ascended diagonally from the west bank.

Two hundred yards further up he made out the gray shape of a huge rock outcropping wherein lay the cave. He set the pack down again and, after fumbling with the zipper, brought out the little pen light, then made his way carefully into the mouth.

Indian Joe had shown it to him in what seemed like a hundred years before—a hidden chamber the Paiutes had used in their wars with the Washos—not tall enough for a man to stand straight in, perhaps four feet wide and ten feet deep, but with a twisting crawl space thru the back, providing the critical second exit. And while he hadn't been there for a very long time, he still remembered the removable stone buried in the sand in the corner, and behind which had been the hide wrapped blanket of rabbit skins, some coiled hemp line and Indian bone fish hooks. With rising excitement, and with something of the anticipation of meeting an old friend, he worked the stone loose. However, though the line and hooks were intact, the skins long since had stiffened and were turning to a powdery dust. So that disappointed, he lay down near the entrance, then didn't feel the cold, even at dawn.

In fact it was mid-morning before he awakened, staring dully out at the sunlit trees and dam below. Just conscious and with his mind barely functioning, getting up after a time from necessity and most cognizant of the great fatigued heaviness in his limbs. Outside the cave he relieved himself, then drank from a small seep and returned inside for a bit of the jerky. Then with more effort, gathered a few armloads of pine needles for a better bed, and lay back inside, dozing in and out of sleep for the duration of the day. In the starlit evening he drank more and ate again, feeling somewhat revived, and even went for a small sortie down to the water's edge before repairing to sleep once more.

Chapter Four

Indian Joe used to tell him about the Indians, often speaking of the Washo Indians, rather than about his own tribe, the Paiutes; and while this seemed strange, given the fact that the Paiutes were fierce and bitter rivals of the Washos, Jeff finally decided it was simply because Joe himself was trying to understand.

Sometimes, too, because of Joe's immersing him in Indian ways, Jeff felt as if the Indians and the land were more parent to him then his own father and mother. In the Tahoe woods he'd feel more Indian then white, and in his mind's eye sometimes could even see the Indians, or at the very least feel their presence.

As soon as the spring weather permitted, the Washo made their annual ascent to the great blue lake "near the sky"—toiling up from the Washo and Carson valleys to the East.

The Washos called the place Da ow a ga, *which means "edge of the lake," though later on the white people mispronounced it so that the Da ow became "Tahoe".*

The great lake was a hundred miles around and was the centerpoint for the Washos' activities. They believed it sacred, that it breathed life into the fish and birds and animals, as well as into the land and plants and people. And because it was sacred, and because the whole tribe came there in summer to reaffirm their unity as a people, the gathering was considered of utmost importance. From all parts of their territory, they came to "bless the waters," then camped as groups in a dozen or more designated areas scattered along the shoreline. Then, their leaders would meet often to establish rules and guidelines and to discuss the many important aspects of the Washos' life.

Fish were abundant in great number in Da ow a ga and included several varieties of trout and whitefish, all of which spawned up the streams along which the Indians camped. Fishing sometimes with hooks and sometimes with willow spears with bone points, with conical basket traps with funnel entrances, with nets strung across the streams and with fish pools made by diversion dams, the men caught what they needed to support their families for the year. After the day's fishing, small and large fish were split open for cleaning; small fish were cooked in coals in woven, coarse baskets, larger fish were wrapped in sunflower leaves and shoved down under the fire and those fish to be used later were set out to dry.

The Indians lived from the land and close to it; they did not abuse it and thus there was abundance. They did not disrupt the reproductive cycles of the fishes, so that from one generation to the next the fish remained.

It was the same with all. None were overhunted—not the deer, nor the groundhogs, nor mountain goats, nor antelope, nor woodchuck, nor prairie dog, nor sagehen, nor quail, nor waterfowl. So that the cycle of life could continue from one year to the next, and on into the distance.

When they killed an animal, they prayed to the Maker, both for providing the food and for forgiveness for taking a life.

From one generation to the next, they passed down the knowledge of the fish, and of the seeds and plants and nuts, so that there was continued a cycle of life unbroken.

The white men, when they came, scorned the Washo and referred to them as "diggers" and "fish eaters," not bothering or perhaps not advanced enough in their own thinking, to applaud the artistic achievement in such a survival. The Washos' range in general was harsh dry desert, Da ow a ga to the contrary, as autumns and winters were spent in the arid hills and valley to the East. There all seeds, bulbs, stalks, leaves and roots were viewed as potential foods or medicines.

Among the many seeds understood, harvested and prepared by the Washo women were cattail, wild mustard, tule root, wild spinach, tiger lily, sego lily, sand seed, wild potato, sweet elderberry, wild rhubarb, gooseberry, chokecherry, wild celery, buckberry, wild turnip, strawberry, currant, raspberry, onion and rose tea.

Adaptation followed adaptation and a whole body of knowledge developed. Certain plants and seeds could be gathered for only short periods, so it was necessary to know exactly when they would mature. Further, while some plants were eaten on gathering, others required various preparations for storing and winter use. Women cleaned the wild seeds in winnowing baskets—which they had woven—then parched the seeds with hot coals and pounded them into flour which would keep for months and could be made into soup or mush.

The Washos gathered pine nuts, one of the most important crops, in the sacred hills to the East. There, a qoom sa bye (five day ceremony) would be held to bless and honor the Maker.

Afterwards, nuts would be picked for up to six weeks, the cones knocked down from the trees

with long, hooked-tip poles, then roasted in slow
fires which would ease the cones open and allow
the nuts to be removed. Women would crack the
shells open with metate and mano shells, then with
winnowing baskets sift the kernels free. These in
turn would be ground into flour and made later into
the staple soup.[2]

He awoke with a start. There was a light in the cave even though it was still night, and instinctively he grabbed for the stick of wood beside him—before recognizing them. They sat shadowed, both with backs propped against the cave wall opposite, regarding him somberly.

The Indian grunted. "You'd have been dead a few times," he said laconically, taking a cigarette out of his shirt pocket and placing it between his lips. But already Jeff's eyes had shifted to his brother.

Tony was thick and swarthy, not as tall as he, but infused with a great bear like strength which seemed to surround his presence. Jeff hadn't seen him for years, but as their gaze locked, there seemed to be no difference. On many things they probably still agreed.

"Well, you did it, eh?" his brother said after awhile, tonelessly.

"Yeah."

The Indian stirred up the fire in the rocks, then hunched back down with a sigh.

"Well, what now?" his brother said, and he could read the question in their eyes.

"Do you mean do I think there's any hope?" he said sarcastically.

"Hold it, Jeff," the Indian shot back. "You know what he means. He means do we hit them again?"

---

[2] JoAnn Nevers, *Wa She Shu: A Washo Tribal History*, Inter-Tribal Council of Nevada, Reno, Nevada, 1976.

He looked at them—both eyeing him, waiting—and he didn't know what to say.

"We?" The question was blurted, coming from somewhere deep in his insides—a window on his alienation.

"You're not the only one in it, you know?" the big Indian said sharply. "Do you think Tony would have come all the way from Alaska if you were?"

He was silent. The dimming lantern showed their faces both deep brown, as they leaned towards him earnestly. 'How he loved them,' he thought; and yet more than ever, he believed their cause so hopeless.

"I guess that's why you went to live in Alaska, huh?" he said to his brother finally, a touch of anger again in his voice. "Because you thought you could do so much from up there."

The words hung in the cave's dank air, stinging; and instantly he regretted them, knowing them unfair, and remembering Tony's circumstances at the time. Besides which they loved him also, he knew, or they *wouldn't* have been there. "Well, why did you start it?" his brother flushed, "if you didn't think it was worth doing?"

"I don't know," he said. "I hadn't seen Glenbrook before."

Then they were all three silent, and the Indian again got up to stir the fire. The limbs sparked and crackled; still, though the thirst for just resolution still smoldered and wanted to flame up, it was nearly smothered by Hamil's dark despair.

"They've called off the search," the Indian said at length. "Claim they've found a leak in a gas line that caused it."

Jeff grunted. "Just means they don't want to have a messy trial when they find me," he said.

His brother's laugh was abrupt, brittle. "My own brother, the folk hero!" he said. "It wouldn't do them a lot of good."

"Yeah." He grinned faintly then, feeling himself relax—stretching his legs out and leaning back farther against the ridged wall. Then like a freshening wind, there came a mood change, very subtle and yet perceptible, and he wondered at it—wondered if it were somehow just the product of Tony's laugh.

"How was it, Jeff?" Indian Joe asked him, the voice softer now; in the flickering fire light, his great hooked nose—so badly disfigured by the police beating—softened, also, though still evident in the grotesque and great shadow reflecting from the cave wall.

And he told them—told of the weeks of careful scouting and planning; of the night itself and the explosion; the long swim and the run thru the forest afterwards. And with the telling, also imperceptibly at first, there was a gaining and, as it played off the two and back to Hamil, his voice grew stronger. They were cheered and, with the positive response, he was surprised to feel the flame again flaring up. It wasn't logical, but it felt right for the moment. Still, something in him clung to the idea he ought to resist it, perhaps not fully reconciled *even now* with the act he'd already committed. 'Why, after all, did it matter anymore anyhow?'

"Well, you hurt them . . . ," the Indian said after a time.

"But?"

"But that's as far as it goes. No one knows why you hurt them. And now most people don't even know that it was *someone* that hurt them. No one knows that you believe the way you do. No one even knows who you are. And we don't know for sure if there's anyone out there who believes the same way anymore at all!"

He paused, leaning forward, his dark eyes gleaming and intense. "If our side is never broadcast, never publicized, never even acknowledged, all this becomes is an isolated act of violence—one man's vendetta against the system."

Jeff looked at him, a great, wounded hulk of a man with glittering black eyes, smiling ruefully and, as always, going to the heart of a matter.

"What I'm saying," he went on, "is you should decide pretty soon what you're going to be. Either you're going to quit now with your one statement that only a few people know about; or you're going to continue on from time to time, acting as a lone wolf and lashing out as it suits you, without any hope of it extending out beyond the mere act itself. *Or.* . . we could all together finally figure out a way to reach others—whether by short wave or commandeering a TV station, or what, I don't know—and conduct the thing as it needs to be conducted, as a war against people who've stolen our land."

He rose, his great girth blocking out the light entirely for a moment, then moved over again to fuss with the fire. And Jeff watched him without vexation, but rather with admiration, and the sense of well being he'd always felt when he was near. There remained for him the problem, though, and the strong statements merely pointed to it.

In the morning he awoke late, with the sun already breasting the eastern ridge and golden rays slanting off the dam's ruffled dark hued surface. And they were gone.

He looked outside the cave, expecting to see them puttering around the rocks, or perhaps down near the shore; but there was nothing, no one, just the light chill breeze carrying the scent of pine, and a lone hawk which hung suspended and near motionless in the upper currents. He sat down heavily then on an old stump and grieved in the depths of his soul, realizing now that they'd never been there and how alone he really was.

Indian Joe, he knew, had been moved from the penitentiary to a hospital for the criminally insane, years before when he'd escaped and tried to blow up Derby Dam—the dam which had brought doom to the Indians' fishery. And everyone said from that hospital, there could be no escape. If they hadn't lobotomized him by then, they would have at least fried his brain with their terrible drugs, he knew, and there could be no hope.

He considered the dream then and what had been said, nonplused by the vividness and able to recall every word and gesture—so that he was sure, too, that his own sanity must be in the balance.

Indian Joe had said they needed to 'conduct a war against those who had stolen their land,' but when he thought about it—about all the changes that had been wrought since he was a boy—it was hard to see the value of winning. He thought of the giant casinos, the highways, the cars and the fetid air; the miles upon miles of motels and hamburger stands, curio shops and pizza parlors. People by the thousands come to work for the casinos—many of them good law abiding, trusting souls, who didn't even suspect oppression, but who owned thousands of houses which now covered the land.

And he thought of their sewage which had polluted the great Lake, covering its once clean rocks with a brown coating of algae, and leaving the once joyously teeming waters mostly dead and devoid of living creatures. So that, he could see no turning back, no recapturing of what was lost, no hope of removing the blight. Even if he and Joe and his brother could blow up all the casinos and all the motels and hamburger stands and pizza parlors, they'd still not be able to get it back to where it had been. And too, the thought kept coming back to him—a memory really—of something a woman from Oakland had been quoted by the newspaper as saying years before when some extortionists had planted a bomb in a casino. "I just can't imagine it," she'd said, "why anyone would want to hurt a casino!"

He sat for a long time with his head in his hands, then after awhile thought again of his brother. Tony had understood better than he, realizing years before—even before he'd had to leave—that the best option was simply to go where it was like it used to be, rather than trying to get things back to what they had been.

Chapter Five

Their father, Ned Hamil helped to start "The League to Save Lake Tahoe." It was a non profit organization made up mostly of concerned Californians who had the foresight—or misfortune—to understand.

And in the beginning, the League was nearly successful. Members bombarded the Nevada and California Capitals and the Courts with their petitions and lawsuits. And legislators in California—the State with the majority of Lake waters within its bounds—responded by creating the Tahoe Regional Planning Agency (TRPA), proposing it become a "Bi-State Compact," wherein both States would have representation, developments would be required to meet strict environmental standards, and the approval of the majority of the "combined" representatives would be necessary before a development could get underway.

Which caused the gamblers and developers on the Nevada side to scramble to cut off the public groundswell of support. Cleverly, thru their shrill mouthpieces in the press, they resurrected old prejudices between the States, succeeding in dividing the public on the issue and, in so doing, buying time. Then, behind the scenes, hammered out their own solution.

'Nevada gladly would join the Bi-State Compact,' they agreed after a time, 'provided her interests were protected by means of a "dual majority" vote.' Which meant that a proposed development could be turned down only if a majority of the delegates in each State voted against it. Thus, if five out of five California representatives voted against an environmentally grievous project, the development would still go forward, as long as only two out of the five Nevada delegates voted against it. Seven *against and three in favor, and yet the "ayes" still had it and the project went ahead—an aberration which nevertheless was exercised time and time again in the ensuing years, as the gamblers' crooked delegates from Douglas, Washoe and Story counties on the Nevada side chose routinely to allow every proposed development at Lake Tahoe to go forward regardless. And when Ned Hamil and his League appealed to the Courts, judges inevitably had the rationale to fall back on that these developments had been 'already studied and approved by the Bi-State Compact.'*

Which was not even to mention the Governor—later to be the great Senator—priming the pump still further by pushing thru the Legislature a provision allowing for "corporate" gaming licenses. Which, while attracting big investment from the East, also removed "all" effective control from the hands of Nevada's people. So that then, any mobster or mobster group could have a gaming license in the name of an upfront corporation, and no one in the State would know who or what they were.

After spending most of the morning with his thoughts, and still half-expecting to see Indian Joe and Tony emerge from the forest, Jeff Hamil roused himself from the stump where he'd been sitting, stretched his still tired and aching muscles and moved back into the cave. There he ate a bit more of the jerky, which seemed even greasier and less appetizing than before, so that afterwards he came away with fresh resolve.

He used the Indian hemp and L-shaped fish hooks from the cave which, also in the way of the Paiutes, he baited with black and white grubs from some greasewood roots.

Then afterwards, he waded in the icy cold water of the dam, down near the end where it emptied into the creek, setting the line (with hooks at intervals) perpendicular to the shore. There, there was greater movement of the water, and then, too, he had had always a peculiar instinct when it came to the whereabouts of fish.

He set the line in the late afternoon and hauled it the next morning, pleased by the result—taking half a dozen plump trout on the dozen or so hooks. He removed the heads and split them down either side of the backbone in the Indian way, removing vertebrate and entrails together, then removing the fins and washing the remaining pink flesh carefully. Afterwards—after making slashes at intervals in the meat to avoid curling—he tied the fish in pairs by the tail and then onto a stretched line out the back side of the cave to dry.

He set several deadfalls in the rocks, too—large, flat stones propped up by a clever triggering device made of four sticks and a bit of line, and baited with pinion nuts—catching in a short while two nice gray squirrels. He didn't know how long he might be there, but resolved to stay for the time at least, while the intensity of the search for him must be at its peak. And knowing he had an adequate supply of food made it less impracticable.

It *was* generally out of the way—too far for the day hikers and reasonably unappealing for campers as well, so that the chances of being seen weren't great. However, since it was so remote, his solitary camping there—should he be spotted—could be questioned. Thus, he decided to take precautions in advance, determining to extinguish the fire each morning, so that smoke would never be visible curling out from the cave; and, also, and in spite of the bother, resolved to wear the pack or at least have it with him at all times during the day—to appear only as a hiker, and never a resident.

In the mornings some deer came just before dawn to drink, shying the first morning at the fresh scent of him, but growing each day more accustomed and emboldened. And watching from the mouth of the cave, he had no desire to hunt them. There were so few now and he was just glad to see them. He was reminded of a time long before when, as a boy, he had gone with his brother and Joe on a camping trip—of finding Joe lying at the edge of a meadow at dawn, watching a small herd in rapt, even religious admiration.

And again he was reminded of the variety of things he'd learned from Joe.

Joe had been family—had been around seemingly always at the time he and Tony were old enough to hunt and fish. He was the adopted brother of Mary their mother—adopted at age seven from the Indian reservation during the Depression days when Mary's father, who'd always been close to the Indians but who already had eight hungry children to feed, still found it in his heart to add one more to their table.

Then later, when he came back from the War in the Pacific, and fighting the Japanese—shell-shocked and confused—he'd come to stay with Mary and Ned Hamil. Becoming to the boys a surrogate dad, teaching them the intimacies of the still wild Western land, while Ned Hamil was consumed with his practice of the law.

Jeff Hamil settled then into an existence of simply fishing, hunting and staying out of sight in the cave; but it was not a life devoid of tension. His mind continued active and troubled, as memories of the bombing itself and the knowledge that he now was a fugitive were with him always—as he'd known they always would be. He wondered if he had a future and even if he wanted one.

He tried not to think of the girl at all, sure he would never, could never, see her again. Still often she would steal into his conscious anyway—in his mind's eye he'd see her in some familiar pose or expression, or something she said would come back, or just a look in her eyes.

At length he would realize he was thinking of her, and would push her away again, in desperation trying to focus his crying spirit on Lake Tahoe, or any other distraction. But now, Tahoe seemed something dead and buried in the past, his passion gone and lifted up in the burning fireball he'd created—replaced by the always and forever bitter aftertaste of the defeat he had to admit. It was, he knew, an occupation of oppressors, with so-called American freedoms contained within very precise boundaries— "don't rock the gangsters' gambling boat, my son, and you shall be free!"—and, while his hatred for them seemed spent now, or at least at a low ebb, he was feeling with each passing hour a subtle resignation settling over him.

He wondered if it were the resignation of death and thought numbly, if it were, he should fight against it. Yet in his spirit he wept, not for himself, but for what was lost—for what had been and for what they all had had and couldn't have again. And having known it once, he thought himself unfit for life now without.

At other times, he thought he now was limited to two choices: one, either hit at them, and hit at them again; or else give it up entirely, wait until the search had died down and escape to Alaska, as Tony had done. There were plenty of fugitives living there, he knew, and many had done far worse than he. But then irrationally, too, he would feel the weakness steal back over him again and, maudlin, would think that he didn't want to be so forever geographically removed from the girl.

In the darkness, feeling himself on the edge of a precipice, he would remember again what a truly extraordinary place Tahoe had been. And then perhaps in trying to re-justify his action, would force himself to remember some more.

Once, in the early light of dawn, he'd shivered in their small boat, partly from the cold and partly from anticipation. Then his father, Ned, had hooked a fish. It came to the surface in a series of lightning leaps, a big topwater trout called a "silverside" and he thought he would burst with pride and excitement when finally his father asked him to net it. He was eight years old, sturdy and well-made, and later that morning Ned actually let him steer the little outboard to another spot on the lake.

The lake was calm that morning, as it was usually before eight or nine o'clock; and, looking over the side and down thru the silver mirror, he could see a myriad of teeming life—tens of thousands of schooling, green-backed minnows, and below them the darker shadows of prowling trout. There, there was a purity of freshness seldom known—a kind of primordial innocence where the two interfacing mediums of air and water seemed to create almost a third environment—so that the moist air was intoxicatingly sweet and caressing to the skin and, in the aerated water just below, swarms of life seemed in celebration. He didn't want to go home and thought he never wanted to be anyplace else, perhaps realizing dimly even then that time spent there in the early days would be the happiest he would ever know.

Ned taught him to swim the summer before, in spite of a deep rooted fear of drowning which had precluded his learning until then. His mother had tried to teach him when Ned was busy with his work, as had also various aunts and friends. But he hadn't trusted any of them enough and it was one of the times when Indian Joe was away. He and Ned swam together after he'd learned, out to an old piling far offshore where nobody else went— where the chilling water dropped away from green to blue and where Ned was his only guarantee of return.

And later, with the passing of years, in the clearing by the little store, and sometimes in among the big pines and cedars by the beach, he'd learned to play baseball—his first love—with teenagers using rocks for bases, no mitts and an old taped bat and ball. He'd lain on the beach with a red haired girl from Santa Monica, named Joanne for most of a summer when he was fifteen—so that afterwards she'd written him letters that he didn't know how to answer. And he won some rowing contests, and went to teenage dances in a rustic old lodge; then, at first without realizing it, was himself victim of the change.

So that now, thinking about it—with Ned gone, and the clear water, and the swarming minnows and trout beneath; the big trees by the beach cut down and the little store and clearing beside it erased and paved over; the lodge and the red haired girl with all her promise vanished—all that remained were the ghosts, and the single piling like himself, which still stood as lonely sentinel far out from the shore.

Chapter Six

He'd called her, asking if they might talk, relieved when she'd agreed and overlooking in the low, quiet voice the strong new resolution. In the warm May twilight, she'd been pretty in yellow shorts and fresh white top; yet again, in the aunt's old car, she was pensive and there was uneasiness between them.

She'd wanted to stop first at a married friend's apartment— to get information about library schedules, she said—and Hamil readily complied, grateful then to have her in anyway in his debt. But then, she used the time to flirt tauntingly with the friend's young husband in a way that left Hamil feeling humiliated and defenseless. He'd tried to make small conversation with the wife but had failed miserably, so that there were long pauses while both listened instead to the husband and Sue Marie.

Still afterwards, again in the car, he said nothing of it, as the cold, hard knot of fear gripped his stomach once more, and he tried to convince himself he wasn't drowning, and that it was just a temporary situation, a lashing out at him for their "non-evening" at Glenbrook.

He took her to a movie—a light, airy thing about the old West—and, sitting next to her in the darkened theater, knew again that he never wanted to be anywhere but beside her. She laughed with the movie and the tension seemed broken; still in his spirit he felt an awaiting dread, which he tried again to set aside.

Afterwards, they'd stopped for pizza in a crowded place where there was much noise and little conversation; and then outside her parents' house in the car, he'd proposed to her, knowing the time was wrong but in panic that she wouldn't see him again if he didn't do something, and unable to think of whatever else would be drastic enough to turn things around.

"Will you please marry me?" he said, struggling to control his breathing and with his arm around her tentatively.

To which her first sudden impulse was a kind of a snort. "No!" she said emphatically, and it was as if she'd long since finished considering it—as if the idea was now preposterous.

The word on the street was that the explosion at Glenbrook was not gang related—that it had been a one man operation—and the word had gone out from the corporate board rooms in Detroit and St. Louis and Chicago, received and relayed in Las Vegas. There was to be no trial when the perpetrator was caught—no glorification of terrorism, nor risk of creating some cult hero who might speak out for the disaffected. Whoever had done the deed needed to be terminated, not recognized; and the newspapers were to report simply, and just as Indian Joe had foretold, that there'd been evidence of a gas leak which had triggered the explosion.

Simultaneously, the regular law enforcement authorities were to announce the calling off of their search—the fictionalized gas explosion serving to explain why no other leads had been found. The populace would settle back into their normal lethargy and, within a day or two, there would be no further speculation as to who had done what or how.

Then the professionals would do their job, the unseen army of paramilitary men, capable, thorough and deadly, who were well paid, equipped and retained for just such eventualities—those messy little jobs which the regular law couldn't handle and still maintain the facade. The system after all had to be protected and perpetuated at all cost, and the existence of the "army" was emphatic evidence of that.

The Governor and all public officials, Senators and Congressman, were notified that the search had been called off— that the explosion was gas related. For if the properly elected officials didn't know, but only suspected, their testimonies could never be turned to disadvantage. And the great Senator himself, who was said to be actually close to the President of the Land, had been shown long ago the wisdom in knowing nothing.

Jeff Hamil had been at the little dam for perhaps a week and a half when he first heard the sound of people, their raucous voices and blaring transistor radio preceding them thru the woods to the South. His gut wrenched as he was hit with sudden panic, thinking to take immediate flight. He looked around wildly for the backpack which was propped against a nearby tree; but then the calm hand of reason brought restraint, as he realized—as at Spooners—who they were not. Lawmen and trackers, he reminded himself again, would not be so indiscreet.

It was past noon and he had been once again resting against the old cut stump by the shore, lazing in the sun and having pulled the fish line hours earlier. The catch which was meager—just three fish and two of them small—he'd already split and hung to dry and he'd long since extinguished the fire as well. Still in his mind, he was in no way prepared to receive visitors of any kind; and for a moment, he thought again of bolting or simply hiding out. But then immediately, it was too late, as he was spotted, and those options were extinguished.

They came thru the trees at the other end, having followed—doubtless ignorantly, he thought—the old Indian trail up from Ash Canyon and Carson City, and then couldn't help but see him, as the lake was small. There were three of them, and one shouted and waved immediately.

"Hey!" he yelled, and Hamil responded desultorily, his half-raised arm reflecting both resignation and despair. Still he didn't know exactly what to do, so continued to sit as he'd been by the water; then in what seemed like no time, they were upon him, surrounding him with their motion and sound.

"Howdy, how's the fishin'?" the tallest one, who was also the first to reach him, greeted. Red cheeked and with a red baseball cap turned ridiculously backwards, he was still huffing and puffing from the hike up—in his mid-thirties, dressed typically in blue jeans and lettered white T-shirt, and with a great large body gone prematurely soft with flab.

He grinned crookedly at Hamil, cocking his head slightly while at the same time raising the can of beer he was carrying in a mock toast. "Say, you one of those hippie fellas, or somethin'? he asked laughingly, still appraising Hamil thru big horned rimmed glasses, peering in such a way as to seem deliberately *over* observant—as if it were in fact required of one who'd chosen to spend his day out of doors—an affected attitude which, nonetheless, caused Hamil to feel suddenly very conscious of his own appearance and the fact that he hadn't shaved in nearly a month.

Still he didn't speak and it didn't seem to matter, as the tall fellow went on. "Just out enjoyin' nature are ya? Well, that's all right. We just hiked up from Carson City," he said. "Heckuva hike! Started about six this mornin' and it must be afternoon by now. Heard from my granddad there was good fishin' up here, but it's the first time I ever made it here myself."

Hamil regarded the others then similarly arrived, winded and perspiring. First, a Mexican, typically short and squat with a smiling moon face, dressed like the other two in jeans, but with a bright blue polo shirt; and afterwards, the third member, a much younger man in a soiled white shirt, pale and with long, unkempt sandy hair, sporting a thin little mustache which merely added to his generally seedy appearance, and with red rimmed hollow eyes giving witness to his obvious addiction. Hamil thought the Mexican, who like the leader was carrying an open can of beer, was probably one of the illegal aliens the clubs were bringing in by the droves—not only willing, but glad to work for less than minimum wage and, because of language problems, not apt to find employment elsewhere—a situation making for stability in the gambling work force, at the same time guaranteeing lower overhead.

"Well, I'm just hiking thru," Hamil said at last, surprised by the unfamiliar sound of his own voice. "Just stopped for awhile to rest." Then, "you all work at the clubs?" He asked with some curiosity, then regretted it immediately as a warning light flashed on too late in his brain. Questions would beget questions, and an intimacy he was not prepared to share.

"Oh yeah," the leader responded with noticeable bored resignation. "It ain't much, but it's a living".

The others nodded their affirmation.

"Doesn't pay much, huh?" Hamil said after a pause, resignedly, knowing himself trapped now into more talk.

"Nah, sometimes I feel like blowing the joint up," the other returned, "just like somebody did over there at Glenbrook."

At which Hamil swallowed, feeling his legs turn suddenly to jelly. He struggled to remain impassive, but the other wouldn't leave it alone.

"You heard about that, didn't you?" the visitor said. "You haven't been out here that long? Got everything but the old inn."

"Well yeah, I heard about the explosion," Hamil responded carefully, grateful nevertheless for the news about the inn. "What they're saying around the Lake, though", he went on, remembering suddenly what Joe had said in the dream and anxious for a diversion, "is that it was a gas main leak."

"Gas main leak!" the other exclaimed. "Well, I heard that, too, but it seems like more of that good old gangster warfare to me." He looked at Hamil directly, though, as he said it—Hamil thought again a trifle suspiciously. And then, blessedly, attention shifted as the Mexican spotted a rising trout.

Then the leader led the way in the feverish stringing of rods, first tossing his empty beer can into a nearby manzanita bush, then unlashing the two sections of fishing pole from the large red, white and blue backpack he'd earlier set on the ground. He fit the two sections together, expertly Hamil thought, then bent to unzip the backpack; and it was then that Hamil saw the gun. It was a black, snub-nosed revolver, set on top along with the spinning reel, which the man drew out to join to the pole; and it was at once, also, fuel for speculation and imaginings. 'Was he really some sort of cop, or just the redneck he appeared to be? And, given the gun, what if any were his inhibitions about using it?'

Hamil sat transfixed while the man brought forth, also from the pack, a fantastically shaped piece of chartreuse hardware called a "goblin" which he in turn affixed to the end of the line.

"So you haven't been fishing here at all, huh?" he asked, Hamil thought again suspiciously. And then, while his companions were still involved in their own preparations, flung the "goblin" mightily thru the air, to a splattering splashdown a good fifty yards from shore. "I bet we can catch us a whole mess of fish here," he said, his eyes narrowed now and watching the water, "if we half try."

He bit his tongue and cranked the reel furiously, twitching the rod tip at intervals and then explaining after the next cast that the faster one reeled, the more action one might expect from a "goblin". "It's ultrasonic," he declared just as a first fish hit. And then simultaneously, his two companions, who were by now fishing with goblins also, had strikes of their own. Then there was much laughing and excitement and, as Hamil leaned back against his stump, watching impassively, they hauled fish after fish out of the water he'd come to think of as his own.

The transistor radio continued to blast country music from its perch on a large nearby rock, so that finally the original peace shattering blasphemy had became the norm. And Hamil, uncomfortable with tension nearly to the point of explosion, wanted nothing so much as to be gone immediately—just to vanish while they were so engrossed. However, the leader continued to worry him, so that he was stuck, thinking a rapid disappearance would further arouse an already suspicious mind.

So, he sat and watched thru an afternoon that he thought would never end—watched as fish that would have fed him for a month were splashed indiscriminately, one after the other to the shore.

An advertisement on the radio caught his attention after awhile, though, and then was repeated several times over—until he'd finally realized its full impact. Then afterwards, it was with him always, so that he didn't ever need to hear it again. It was an ad for a new, paddle-wheeling tourist boat at Lake Tahoe, named of all things, *The Tahoe Dixie*; and the girl in the commercials said a person could catch it and see all the "historic" sights from Zephyr Cove to Emerald Bay. Then the music played, with mocking banjos and cornpone country voices, his father Ned's favorite "Dixie" tune—only with different words:

> "Oh, I wish I were on a ship called Dixie
> Out on a Lake they call Tahoe
> Sail away, sail away, sail away Dixie ship
>
> On the Dixie ship I'll make my stand
> To drink and dine on Tahoe

Away, away, we'll sail away on the Dixie."

He was transported, thinking about Ned whistling the tune to them when they were small boys—when they didn't yet understand his Southern roots, but did understand his joy. And, he thought how Lake Tahoe had been so much a part of that joy. It built in him throughout the afternoon, the insane little ditty repeating over and over in his mind. So that in the end, he didn't care about anything else at all, except getting at them again.

After a couple of hours, when the bite was off, his unwanted companions paused for lunch, sitting on rocks and stumps nearby, pulling sandwiches and more beer from their packs and talking loudly about those they'd caught and those which had gotten away.

"Best darn fishin' I've seen in awhile!" the leader exclaimed loudly, afterwards swigging his beer also with enthusiasm.

"This is the best!" the Mexican agreed. "This and Lake Tahoe."

"Lake Tahoe?" the leader snorted. "There's no fish there!"

"Oh, because it is so beautiful!" the Mexican enthused, his round face shining.

"Used to be fish in Tahoe, though," Hamil blurted suddenly, uncharacteristically. "Plenty of them—fed the Washoe Indians for generations!"

"Indians!" the leader spat. "Fat lot they know about fishin'! Say, sure you won't have something to eat or a beer with us. I've got a couple more beers."

"No," Hamil returned, "thanks, I ate already."

"Say, what do you do for a living, yourself?" The question, too, was abrupt and caught him flatfooted; and though asked in a friendly manner, still he felt his stomach tighten as he searched quickly for an answer.

"Well, I'm a musician," he lied finally, wondering if they'd noticed how long it'd taken him. Still, even if he weren't hiding out, he would have shied from talk of the unpopular war he'd returned from and his subsequent unemployment.

"A musician, eh? Where do you play?"

The question was friendly, interested; still he was wary.

"Oh, at Tahoe," he said. "All around Tahoe." Now, the little ditty was intensifying again in his mind, though, and as a new picture began to take shape—a picture of shocking clarity—momentarily he let down his guard. "Ever play at Harrah's?" the leader asked him.

"Oh yeah, I've played at all of them at one time or another," he said. And then suddenly he was aware of what he'd done, his words hanging there in the air, but not so that he could reach out and take them back.

"Well, I've got a cousin, Ben Jones, that's been playing there at Harrah's forever. I'm sure you must know Ben."

He stared blankly for a moment, then tried lamely to explain. 'He'd never played Harrah's for more than a night or two—filling in when somebody got sick—so that he'd never really learned names.' And all the time he was explaining, he was reading new doubt on the leader's face, and thinking what a phony they now must all believe him to be.

"Well, just in case he remembers you, who shall I tell him you are."

"Oh, sorry!" he said. "Tony . . . , Tony Joseph." And then, as an afterthought, "I didn't catch your name either."

"Howard Johnson."

"Hello, Howard," he said, smiling falsely and taking a step forward from his stump to shake the slowly extended hand of the standing Johnson.

"Say Howard", he said, "I think I'll be heading out soon. I've got some ground to cover."

"Yeah, well you might just as well stay the night with us," was the response into which Hamil now read all sorts of ill defined jeopardy. "You know there's no civilized place you can get to now, not before dark."

"Well yeah," Hamil said, feeling himself ever more in a dangerous game of cat and mouse, and aware, too, of the darkening forest and lengthening shadows on the lake. "but once I get to Marlette, I can find my way in the dark no problem."

"You been up here that often, huh?" Howard Johnson asked, once again curious.

"Ever since I was a kid," he smiled.

He shouldered the pack then, anxious to be gone; still he hesitated for a moment, wishing there was some final word or gesture to allay the unease he was feeling.

"Well ok, Howard," he said finally, "hope I'll run into you all again sometime!"

"Yeah sure," Howard said, already busy tying on a new *goblin*, "see ya."

He headed off on the trail then, thinking he'd slip around to the back side of the cave for a final, quick tidying up; then heard their voices following him thru the trees.

"Strange dude, that one," the leader said.

"Yeah," the Mexican responded, "I think he's a man got some trouble."

"Yeah, it's strange he'd be all the way up here and not fishin'."

Chapter Seven

For him, her rejection had been the end of all things. He'd walked along the river in the night, curling up finally in a hollow, below a gnarled old willow and listening to the water's gurgling— running things over and over in his mind until the early dawn light in the East brought with it the settling cold.

Then, he walked again to generate heat, gaining strength with the growing light, thinking maybe it was not over—thinking if he just waited several weeks they might start again on a separate footing.

But, he thought of her incessantly, obsessively, every waking hour for the next two weeks, actually feeling her beside him sometimes, sharing his thoughts and even touching him occasionally with her approval. So that, he thought their spirits somehow were still together, even if physically they were not. He even basked sometimes in knowing that she loved him, and more than ever he loved her, awaiting with a growing eagerness the time when he would see her again—an eagerness tinged after a couple of weeks with odd new shadings of fear. He didn't know what it was, but began to worry that he was waiting too long; still he forced himself to hold off a bit longer, and then was devastated by the dream.

He awoke in a cold sweat with his heart pounding, having seen himself inside a darkened room without any door, and with water rising around his ankles, and strange candelabras falling and igniting wicker furniture. In desperation, he looked for a way out, but there was none—no doors or windows of any sort; and then, too, there was the unmistakable feeling of eternity—that this was to be his fate forever.

Shakily he got up and, after dressing hurriedly, left his apartment and began to walk. Again it was just growing light in the East and he walked at first without aim; then, as he found himself in her neighborhood, decided to walk by her house. He knew there was the risk, if he were discovered, of seeming strange. But he thought at five in the morning there was little chance of being spotted; besides he was left with a lingering unease from the dream, which he felt only her proximity could somehow heal. He turned the corner and walked by her house on the opposite side of the street, comforted at first by the sight of her little green car parked in front, and not immediately registering the still burning front porch light.

Then in the late afternoon, at the edge of a meadow where a tiny spring bubbled forth from the rocks to give life to the few struggling animals of the surrounding desert, it hit him—laying beside some sagebrush, head cushioned on his arms and gazing up at the clouds, which scudded rapidly across the deep blue backdrop of the sky.

He'd come to the place before to think. It was a drive from town and then a long hike—at a higher elevation where scattered pine trees could be seen but chances of seeing anybody were remote. Here, he thought he could breathe and get in touch with himself again, also perhaps come to understand the strange, empty void which he'd felt since the dream.

He'd been there for he didn't know how long—long enough to watch little, almost invisible birds flutter down to the spring to drink, and to see a black skunk come bounding halfway cross the meadow, only to scent him and bound back the way he'd come. He turned his head slowly and then was suddenly transfixed. For some reason, his gaze became riveted on a strange, almost bizarre-looking plant known as "desert thistle". Two of three tall prickly stocks were topped with bract-protected purplish flowers, but the third was faded and withered—deflowered, as it were. And suddenly, unexplainably but terribly, it swept over him, unhinging his sanity. Struck down, in a rush he remembered her blushing reference to "personalized" instruction and realized the connection with the dream and the front porch light and the void.

Out of view of Hobart and the fishermen, he struck off North and West, ignoring the return trail South to Marlette Lake; then at dark, troubled by thoughts of Howard Johnson and the gun he'd seen, camped cautiously in amongst some large black boulders and without fire, eating the remaining dried fish he'd salvaged from the cave. He slept fitfully, then not at all, hearing the re-playing plagiarized music; thinking of Ned, his father; and considering the new plan crystallizing in his mind.

There was a greatness in Ned's life of losing struggles, and he thought of it as a grand and glorious patchwork quilt that had been made from rags.

Ned represented clients in personal injury cases against the casinos—losing battles which other attorneys wouldn't touch—cases replete with rigged judges and juries and a whole community of cowardly doctors, who under pressure from the mobsters would lie on the witness stand, refuse to cooperate or simply be "out of town" when needed.

Ned fought to prove the complicity of the gamblers and the electric company in rigging public rates to finance the casinos' electrical power, and endured the newspapers' relentless ridicule for charging that the casinos were skimming off profits to avoid paying taxes. He tried to prevent the gamblers from having the new super highway routed thru the peaceful old part of town, near the university and beside the hospital, for the sole purpose of bringing *all* interstate travelers within the bright lights' allure. And, he tried to help Indian Joe's Paiute Tribe obtain their rightful share of water to preserve the reservation's historic Pyramid Lake.

But what came back to Jeff over and over again in his musings was not something Ned had done specifically, but rather an image that his mind somehow had conjured—a picture of Ned standing with folded arms and with Lake Tahoe behind him, facing the devouring giant which others refused to recognize.

Ned Hamil, the little Southerner who somehow saw Lake Tahoe more for what it was, than did those who'd always been there—representing the foredoomed League to Save Lake Tahoe at forever meetings, hearings and appeals. Always idealistic, always believing one man could make a difference—as if, in fact, Nevada were like any other place in America. Mounting his own one man

49

campaigns, writing letters to the Governor, legislators and newspapers, Urging that the State buy property for Tahoe parks, and taking money from his own pocket to pay for his impassioned radio speeches.

Alone, in the thirties, right after he'd come to Nevada and on his first visit to the Lake, naively diving off the end of Glenbrook pier on a sunny day in mid-October and being instantly baptized. Saying many times afterwards, it was as if his scalp and face and chest and arms and groin and legs had been set afire with cold; and from that moment of near hyperventilation forward, being forever in love with the Lake and committed to its preservation.

At dawn Jeff Hamil struck the trailhead leading down and out to the North end of the Lake, stopping twice only briefly to drink from streams, and reaching the little village at Incline in the late afternoon. Bearded and with his pack on his shoulder, appearing still as any late summer hiker and, in spite of his apprehensions, drawing scarcely a glance as he passed down the sidewalk in front of several shops and entered a booth to phone. It would be the second time in as many months that he'd called his friend, Miller, who worked in an armory in L.A. Miller was in ordnance now but had been, besides himself, the sole survivor from their company in Vietnam.

"Same drop zone?" the voice on the other end was terse, military and matter of fact.

"Yeah, by the old tree again would be fine."

"Probably won't get it there for a couple of days. My pickup's out of service till then."

Once he and Miller had blown up a bridge together on the Ho Chi Minh Trail, then had spent three weeks cut off behind enemy lines, out of radio contact and running from the North Vietnamese regulars, the Viet Cong, the Russians and just about everybody else, it seemed. And once Miller, at a party after they'd gotten back, had suddenly grabbed a loaded .22 rifle off a mantel and pumped a hail of bullets into a wall, perfectly outlining the body of his girlfriend—a peace protester named Gretchen—as she stood petrified against it. So that afterwards, they hadn't dated anymore.

"Hey Hamil, uh, you ok? I mean . . . you gonna make it?" The voice had changed and was suddenly anxious.

"Yeah." he said.

And three days later, on Saturday, he slipped thru the forest on the California side, cautiously approaching the scarred old tree where Miller had made the previous drop. It was at the edge of a faintly defined logging road; and, though there was an adjoining clearing, it had always been remote, removed as it was several miles to the South of the Lake. He moved quietly, carefully thru the forest—out of habit by now; still he didn't bother to wait for night, so confident was he that no one would be around.

Thus, the shock was intense when he found the clearing filled with young children playing ball. The sounds of their shouting echoed thru the trees, stopping him in his tracks; so that afterwards he proceeded with great stealth—slipping from tree to tree after long, careful watching— until he could confirm that the worst was true.

Twelve or fourteen kids had set up bases in the clearing and were playing softball—some girls as well as boys. And more importantly, several picnicking parents were there, also, chatting and looking on from the sidelines. So that, he thought first of just going away and hoping no one would find the bag Miller had left. From his vantage point in among pines and brush, he could see the tree plainly, perhaps fifteen yards removed from where they'd set up home plate; and he thought if he were gone and someone did find it, 'what would it really matter?' They couldn't trace it to him, and he was sure Miller would have covered his tracks, also, careful not to leave prints and doubtless having scratched off any serial numbers.

But then, he couldn't leave, and the reason was that he'd already set his mind. Now, just as before at Glenbrook, he'd become clear headed and focused, eschewing any more self examination. And, also, he felt as if he couldn't ask Miller again if something went wrong.

So, he continued to stand in hidden among the clustered trees with the fresh sweet scents of pine and sagebrush intermingling all around him, hoping no one would come over towards the tree and watching and waiting for an hour, then almost two. Finally though, one boy of about eleven, growing increasingly bored with the game, wandered unerringly thru the brush and stumbled right over the bag. He was slender, with flashing black eyes behind horn rimmed lenses and a long, thin Pinocchio nose. Wearing a bright yellow T-shirt, and shorts with one leg green and the other yellow.

"Hey, what's this?" he exclaimed, bending immediately to pick it up. Then louder, "Hey Dad, look at this!"

At which point, Hamil couldn't wait any longer, moving quickly to appear at the boy's side—lifting the green issue duffel bag by the handle up and away.

"That's something I had to leave off here this morning, son," he said. "Don't mind me collecting it now."

But the dad was on the scene then, too, a chunky blonde man with crew cut hair and glinting gray eyes, dressed also in shorts and a pastel checkered shirt.

'Ex-military,' Hamil thought, 'without a doubt!'

"You're sure that's yours, buddy?" the man said in a twangy voice, and with a kind of reflexive defending of his son's interest, even though the son had no claim.

"Yeah, I'm sure," Hamil muttered, aware once more of his wild, unkempt appearance, and turning away abruptly towards the trees.

However, he'd not gone more than a step when Pinocchio's voice again rang out thru the clearing: "Well, what's in the bag anyway, Mister, drugs?" he shouted. At which Hamil stumbled slightly, then managed to keep on, feeling many eyes on him, but not at all anxious to prove he had no drugs in the bag by showing off the bombs. Thus, he vanished quickly into the trees, but with the belief that he'd soon be reported.

He set a blistering pace thru the woods, working off towards the mountains oppositely from the way they'd seen him go, trotting and running in spite of the bag, which he finally discarded after transferring the contents to his pack. He traveled all night, then holed up in the day; and an hour past midnight on the following night, filtered ghostlike thru the little meadow North of Zephyr Cove beach, the home port of the "Tahoe Dixie."

She was moored at the end of the long lighted pier; and he lay in the darkness without moving at the water's edge, able to see only one guard, a night watchman stationed in a little guard shack up near the main gate. Beyond that, there was the rustic old restaurant and lodge, now darkened, and close by some scattered houses and summer cabins.

He waited for what seemed like a long while, until the dark figure of the guard emerged from the shack and walked out on the dock to the boat—shining his flashlight about in a cursory manner before returning the way he'd come. And Hamil marked the time on his watch, then waited some more until the procedure was repeated in precisely an hour—then believed he understood enough.

'An hour should be long enough,' he thought; and, without delaying further, stripped down to his dark shorts, shivering slightly in the evening cool. Then he pulled a miniature black inner tube from the backpack, which he'd set beside him on the ground, and inflated the float with small, careful puffs, mindful of how sound carried over water. Once at Glenbrook, he'd spotted a deer on a far point after first hearing its snorting—something that had happened on an autumn morning a very long time before, but the memory of which now brought again the familiar tightening in his chest, so that he had to force it from his mind.

He tied a piece of twined webbing in the tube's center hole and set the tube floating in the shallow water, then carefully removed the three limpet mines one by one from the pack and cradled and tied them in the netting—hurrying in the darkness with a growing sense of urgency, but still remembering to set the mine with the timer and two connecting wires on the top. Then afterwards, eased himself tentatively into the chilling water.

He swam soundlessly, pushing the dark float ahead of him, first to a group of large boulders looming up obscurely above the surface, perhaps fifty yards from shore. There he treaded water briefly, carefully watching the ferry again, the dock and, beyond it and just barely visible, the guard's post. When he was six, his father had brought him there on their first fishing trip ever, rowing them out to the same rocks in a leaky little rental boat. Then a large brown trout in the clear waters had stolen his bait, an event he'd witnessed with a pounding heart, but which had been missed by Ned and therefore not entirely believed—a happening that he remembered always with a certain bitter sorrow.

From the rocks it was a quarter of a mile to the end of the dock and his target, but a bit longer swim if he were to stay outside the circle of the pier's light. Still as ever, swimming came so naturally to him that he scarcely thought of it, moving with a strong, silent frog kick thru the murkiness of water and air, the sky dark but for the retreating stars and with the Lake itself a seeming dark void, the almost imperceptible rise and fall of which were still pilot to the inner rhythms of his soul.

He swam and then, before very long, he was there, directly offshore of the stern, and with the "Tahoe Dixie" herself looming up as a shield between him and the watchman's station. It was a monstrosity really, the "Tahoe Dixie," its very name a contradiction—in reality an old barge, with a square built-on passenger cabin and above that a squared off wheelhouse, bracketed by twin black smoke stacks. It was painted a gleaming white with red trim and from a distance, with its absurd fake paddlewheel, actually did resemble a Mississippi riverboat that somehow had lost its way. And Hamil, on close inspection, thought he could sink it easily, and with no great remorse for having done in some great old lady of the sea.

He looked for the glow of his watch dial and saw that twenty-five minutes had passed, thinking if he could attach the charges within the next half hour, with the timer set for thirty minutes beyond that, the explosion should come in the middle of the watchman's cycle, and while he was most likely in the shack and away from the pier.

Chapter Eight

He'd taken her after the fact on a last date to the old ghost town of Virginia City. And on the surface at least, for awhile it seemed better—better than ever. He noticed the tension seemed gone out of her, and it was as if he didn't worry her as before.

When he went to pick her up though, and her mother called her out of her room, he was struck for a fleeting moment by something different in her appearance. It was as if—in his mind's eye perhaps—she momentarily disassembled, so that instead of seeing all of her, he was seeing a nose, an ear, a mouth.

But then, it had passed and she was back together whole and new. In the car, they were able to make small talk and she seemed, he thought, actually glad to be with him—perhaps to be meeting him on another level.

Time passed swiftly, and then they were in the old mining town, strolling loudly on the mostly deserted board sidewalks, past the ancient, seedy buildings and honkytonk saloons—which overlooked the great mounds of mined tailings and boasted only of glories past.

In the charm of the hundred year old restaurant on the hill, she was glowing and had again, unexplainably, that warm melting look for him that didn't need to be translated into words. He told her more about the wonderful things he had seen, not just in the Sierras, but also in Asia—taking care again not to mention the negatives. And for awhile it was as if they were safe in a time warp where nothing bad could get them; and for awhile, too, he was able to forget what he'd learned.

After dinner though, again in the car, suddenly, inexplicably he destroyed it, and it could never, ever be the same.

"You know, I had this dream," he heard himself blurting suddenly, and his life hung there on his words. He looked into her now warm brown eyes, as she waited expectantly, and didn't know what made him do it—whether it was out of his deep seated frustration, need for revenge, or what. He couldn't switch gears, and then he was telling her—about the inescapable room without doors, his walk by her house, the turned on porch light, and the thistle.

Not that he told her with malice. In fact, there was in his voice even a certain wonderment, as to how he'd "been shown" his conclusion. Still then, it didn't matter.

Like the shattering of glass, the spell was broken, and for the last time he would see her soft look harden into stone. Exposed and chagrined by his intrusion into something which was to have been forever most private, she lashed out. "I never want to see you again," she said thru clenched teeth, and there was in it a finality which his dying pleadings on her doorstep could never change.

He swam slowly, carefully, like a piece of flotsam, thru the light which fanned out over the water from the pier's end—bobbing gently, barely moving, while every nerve in his body was shrieking for him to take cover, to hurry for the shadows. With ice water all around him, though, he maintained; and then after a time, he was underneath the shadow of the paddlewheel apparatus (which turned for the tourists' benefit, while underneath twin screw propellers did the actual labor).

He paused for a moment, one hand against the metal hull, and the other steadying the inner tube, feeling the chill creep up from his legs into his back, and then the beginning of a shiver, initially from the cold, but also from the spilling over of his excited nervous energy. He bit his lip, and then tried to screw down hard on his insides to remain in control, knowing how much harder any underwater task became with hands that weren't steady.

He turned his attention deliberately, almost slowly, then to the float; and, pushing it ahead of him, eased out from the paddlewheel and along the port, or outboard side of the vessel. There, away from the light and screened by the tall ungainly craft, he could work in shadow, the black rubber inner tube, with its equally dark passengers, blending in obscurity.

He paused nearly amidships, with his free hand exploring the chipped away paint on the cold, steel hull. Then after pulling the float's tow line, affixed its small magnetic clip to the side of the vessel. So that afterwards, he could work without worrying that the inner tube might float away. He reached into the webbing to untie the first mine (with the timer and connecting wires), afterwards hoisting it up out of the float. And though it weighed only four pounds, was forced nevertheless to kick his feet more strongly beneath the surface to keep his head above the water.

He held onto the side of the boat with one hand, feeling for finger-holds in the cracked paint, while with his other hand clutching the bomb against the side of his body. He breathed deeply a number of times to fill up with oxygen, again watching and anxious that the guard might have heard splashing. Still there was nothing—only stillness to match the quiet water, as even the small sailboats moored near the dock seemed not to move—so that he even thought a little more movement of the water might have been a good thing. Chance splashings would be better muffled; still, on the other hand, large waves or a running current would have made his task more difficult in other ways.

Now after one final breath, he pushed with his free hand against the inward curve of the hull and forced himself under. It was very dark but, by scissor kicking and easing himself along the hull with his free hand, he was able to stay right up underneath, soon finding the keel and then pressing the pie-shaped charge up against it until the magnets took hold. Then he grasped one of the two dangling wires and, bringing it after him, pulled himself back out and up to the surface.

He controlled a gasp as his face broke thru, still disciplined in spite of his anxiety and the cold which by now had invaded his bones. He again searched the stillness without noting any signs of life, the dock empty above and the only sound an intermittent creaking as, pulled by some small and otherwise undetectable current, the "Dixie" tugged at her lines.

Now feeling rather than seeing, he attached the end of the wire he'd brought to the pointed terminal post on the front side of one of the two mines remaining in the inner tube—afterwards untying the knot holding the limpet in the webbing and lifting it out, as he'd done with the first. This time he didn't go under the boat, however, but merely pressed the mine against the hull just under the waterline. He pulled on it to test the strength of the magnets, then satisfied with the placement as well—that it was just outside the starboard side fuel tank—swam easily back to the float for the last and most difficult.

He lifted the mine out and inched back along the side of the ferry until he'd again located number two; then after another series of deep breaths, cradled the last mine with his left arm and found the wire leading from number two back down under the keel to number one. He swam down, following the wire as it fed thru his right hand; then once beneath the keel, was forced to kick harder to keep himself up and to prevent the mine from taking him too deep. He felt where the wire joined the first mine, then feeling carefully found the second wire which was still dangling. He grasped it, thinking to take it with him to the surface, but then a stab of panic seized him, as claustrophobic in the darkness and with his lungs bursting, he was suddenly unsure of direction. He needed air and had precious little time to try to find it, shooting up towards the surface, but angling too steeply, so that his shoulder caught the hard edge of the underside. It bruised him, jolting him to a stop— so that momentarily stunned, he started to sink back down, terrified by his juggling and nearly losing the mine.

He struggled then to get back to the surface, not knowing if he were still directly under the boat or not, and afraid of hitting his head or being trapped underneath. Still there was no way he could ease into it. He had to have air immediately and, swimming upwards, raised his right arm above his head for protection, his hand still clasping the end of the second connecting wire.

Then suddenly, his head burst thru the surface, between the hull and the dock, and right where he needed to be. He gasped, notwithstanding the sound it made, and for the instant even uncaring and only grateful—for a fleeting lucid moment in fact presented again with the choice.

He blocked it from his mind immediately, though, as control returned. And then it was necessary to attach the wire to the third limpet—the one he'd been carrying—and, bracing the mine against one of the dock's pilings, he fought against the cold. He was shaking and had to force himself to work slowly, unable to see underneath the dock's overhang and screened from the pier's light. And then too, incomprehensibly, he thought of her, wondering briefly what she'd think of him now, if she knew where he was and what he was doing—what she'd really think if she considered it all and didn't merely mouth some wretched "peace at any price" cliché, spawned in the reflexive jerking of her knee. Angered then like some wounded animal —like he'd been sometimes in the war—and so that he felt himself able to focus some seemingly uncommon strength, he worked with his legs wrapped around the cold sliminess of the pile, twisting the wire hard in the groove at the base of the mine's terminal; then with his hand feeling like a club, still managing a little locking twist over the top.

Afterwards he turned back to the boat and pressed the now connected limpet against the hull, just below the waterline and outside the fuel tank as he'd done on the other side, knowing the three mines thus placed would achieve maximum damage, resonating together and imploding with the pressure of the water rather than exploding out against it.

And now finished, and with the break in concentration, he felt immediately an intense, almost unbearable nervousness to be away. Taking several more hurried breaths, then swimming quickly one last time back down along the second wire to the controlling mine on the keel. In the darkness, he explored the pie shape, lightly feeling where the wire connected to the terminal, and then just above it and to the right the activating knife switch for the timer which he'd already set. He threw the switch quickly, hearing the satisfying and loud under-the-water *snap*, and knowing then that he had only some thirty-five minutes until the blast. He swam back up to the outboard side, again poking his face thru and into the warm and ordered starlit night—only to be stopped immediately and dead still by the echoing footfalls on the dock. It was the guard, on schedule with the hourly check. Still, an instant kernel of doubt caused him to wonder, and he shrank back, feeling the taper of the keel against his shoulder. He gritted his teeth, trying to control his shivering, as well as his pounding heart, then heard the steps stop just on the opposite side of the boat.

He could feel, or imagined he could feel, the sweep of the flashlight beam over the hull. Then there was nothing —nothing at all—as up above, the watchman paused to light a cigarette, to regard the stillness of the Lake and the stars. Three, four, five minutes went by; and for Hamil, each one seemed infinitely longer than the last. What could it be? Had the man seen or heard something? Could he have spotted the empty inner tube snugged up against the side of the boat?

He clung to the vessel's cracked paint with fingers like claws, wondering what to do if he were discovered there; then after several more minutes, considered with even more dismay the possibility of the guard's simply staying where he was and doing whatever he was doing until it was time for the bombs to go off. Then, he knew he'd have to swim back down and de-activate; there'd be no other choice. And with the guard standing on the dock, or on the boat just above, he knew his chances of escaping detection would be minimal at best.

He waited bleakly, unable to control the shivering now and afraid the guard might detect vibrations from it thru the hull, or spot the little ripples he was causing in the water. He tried to hold his breath and stop the shaking, concentrating on gripping with his hands and straining his ears, also, to try to catch some clue of what was going on. He thought he couldn't stand the cold any longer and then at one point even entertained fleetingly the idea of just striking out, swimming away and being done with it.

Finally though, it came—the first heavy footfall of the guard's departure—and with it unspeakable relief. So that again, he had to restrain himself from leaving too soon. Now, he could see the man up above on the pier, walking away from him and in towards the beach—an old man moving very slowly—leaving the dock at last and crossing a portion of paved parking lot before once again entering his heated booth.

And then Hamil could begin, knowing that now it was less than thirty minutes. He swam stiff with cold and afraid of cramping, stroking still slowly and near imperceptibly as the minutes ticked by—back along the shadow line to the stern, then straight offshore beyond the circle of light. Where finally, he was able to switch to the crawl and knife thru the water without further thought to detection.

In ten more minutes he reached shore, half stumbling and half crawling thru the shallows, near hypothermia and now unmindful of the sounds of his splashing. Immediately he found his clothing, moccasins and pack—piled in the aspen where he'd left them—and, despite the uncontrollable shivering, managed to dress quickly. Then, he hurried in a circular route, half running, half walking thru the trees and meadow, back around to the guard's station, knowing it would be the safer course to flee at once, to slip off thru the woods and cover as much ground as possible *before* the blast, but then reminding himself that it still wasn't about killing little people.

He approached the gate, staying carefully to the shadows and thinking to go undetected unless absolutely necessary. In three or four minutes the bombs would blow, he knew; and, as long as the guard stayed in the booth until then, he'd be all right.

But then suddenly, he saw the door fling open and the guard hurry out, almost as if propelled. And, while in the calm and quiet, it seemed impossible that some suspicion suddenly had motivated it, still it would have been difficult for Hamil to assume anything else. Nor did it really matter that the old man was merely going to retrieve the cigarette lighter he'd laid down on the boat. With his next visit to the vessel not due for another twenty-five minutes, he didn't hesitate, but turned immediately to the dock. So that with the blast imminent, Hamil couldn't wait.

"Hey!" he yelled. "Hey, Mister Watchman, hey, over here!" Not knowing if his slurred speech made him sound like a drunk, but sure that at three a.m., it had to be startling.

And immediately, the watchman stopped in his tracks and turned. He took a step, then flashed his light as Hamil, now out from the shadows, advanced toward the gate.

"What is it?" The watchman approached warily from the other side, and Hamil could see he was wearing a fake dark uniform and cap to make him look like a regular policeman.

"I'm just wonderin'," Hamil called, "what time I can get a ride on that there steamboat?"

At which point, the force of the blast sent them both reeling.

"Holy . . . !" the guard stammered, turning the light away from Hamil then and starting to run back for the booth and the telephone. And in that instant, Hamil was running as well, back into the shadows and the trees, having saved the old man's life all right, but having very much jeopardized his own. The guard had seen his face and a composite would be drawn up; but more importantly, they would know now immediately that the boat's sinking was no accident and would start their manhunt with no delay.

Chapter Nine

After the white men came, in fifty years, a way of life which the Washos had preserved for 10,000 years was no more. Whites stole and claimed the lands, and destroyed the plentiful fish, game and timber.

Miners flocked in the gold and silver rush to the Comstock, in the heart of the Washo territory. And soon the "rush" brought traders and settlers to the land as well.

The pine nut trees were cut down to build homes and stores, and to shore up the mines; and hordes of men who cut them down also trampled plants, destroyed seeds and drove away game. Grazing cattle further destroyed the seeds, which had served to bridge over from one pinenut harvest to another; and at Da ow a ga, white commercial fishermen and (later) resort owners virtually excluded the Indians altogether.

The Washo, a peaceful people, regarded all of this in silence, and in time combined new styles with traditional customs. White man's dress was adopted, the men with Levis and colored shirts and the women in long dresses, shawls, aprons and head scarves.

Now, they lived near towns and ranches where, when they were fortunate, they might find work as domestics or, on occasion, some charity. Then, because their numbers dwindled so drastically from disease, the government decreed a reservation would not be "required."[3]

---

[3] JoAnn Nevers, Wa She Shu: A Washo Tribal History, Inter-Tribal Council of Nevada, Reno, Nevada, 1976.

He didn't know the country to the East beyond Zephyr Cove like he knew Glenbrook, so that in the darkness his movements were less sure. First, there was a labyrinth of riding trails, leading up from the old stables, switching back and interconnecting in a frustrating maze—so that feeling himself going in circles, he soon struck out independently thru the rocks and manzanita brush, climbing directly and preferring to trust his instincts.

Here there were many trees, also—tall, old sugar pine, thrusting up in the gloom to the right and left, and in front of him. While after the first summit, there were many blind canyons and ravines as well—places where he might have holed up, had he not been detected initially. However now, he needed to be far away fast, he knew, so far that they wouldn't believe it possible; and it was to this thought that he tried to cling.

He ran and stumbled and ran again, but now underneath there was something missing—so that sometime, just after dawn, he stopped to understand. He didn't care anymore, he realized, didn't care if he died or not, and didn't see any hope in living. It didn't matter that he'd blown up the boat; didn't matter that he'd blown up the development at Glenbrook; and wouldn't matter what else he might blow up in the future. They'd won. They'd always won. And one last time it came to him: no matter what he did to them, there could be no going back to what it used to be. For Time was like that—blind and relentless and inexorable, favoring no one and anyone. And in that he was fighting Time in concert with *them*, his efforts could be only doomed to frustration. The new people coming to Tahoe, who were ignorant of the past, thought the idyllic was now—in comparison to where they'd come from, or to what would come about later on. And as the old who remembered the past died away, so too did the memories, the root force of their resistance.

He sat for a long while in a patch of black granite boulders, resting; then afterwards when he started again, his pace was slowed and steady. He hiked ever upwards, thru the pines and shiny green manzanita into the high meadows, but it was as if he didn't see any of it, for the fire had gone out.

Around noon, a helicopter flying low and fast came up over the ridge behind, sweeping just above the tree tops and then flashing over the bright yellow meadow which he'd halfway crossed. He stopped and watched as the black and white craft banked, then set down just ahead of him. And then before the rotor blades had stopped turning, one of the two men from inside bounced down, wearing a black jumpsuit and pointing at him what looked like an M-16 rifle with a bayonet.

"Get your hands up!" the no nonsense voice snarled and slowly Hamil complied.

A second man descended from the chopper as well and, armed with a pistol, joined the first as both approached—the second fair skinned and red haired in soiled white coveralls and a counterpoint to his short and swarthy, black clad leader.

"Just keep'em up high!" the swarthy one said, raising the gun to point it at Hamil's head, and while the taller one came around behind to frisk for weapons.

"He's clean," the red head announced, to which the other merely grunted. "Better check the pack."

Hamil removed it as he was ordered and eased it down on the ground camouflage colored, flat and empty now with the bombs, cord and float gone out, but still, he knew, with a little bit of detcord left from before. Numbly, he wished he'd removed it, but then lapsed back immediately into the peculiar torpor which had been with him throughout the day.

Squatting in the yellowing grass, the young white clad pilot undid the straps and the zipper, then in another moment held up the contents in triumph.

"Hey, look here," he said. "What have we got here?"

"Detcord!" the swarthy one replied. "Just what we're lookin' for. Tie him up and we'll give a shout."

Again the tall man came up close behind while the other continued to hold the gun, and for just a fleeting moment *she* crossed his mind again and, in that moment, he thought of trying— even thought he might pull it off. But then it was past, and he sank back still again.

The man tied his hands very tightly behind him, the cords cutting into his wrists; and then, looping another line around his ankles, jerked his feet out from under him, so that he fell awkwardly in the grass. Then his feet were bound equally tightly, as the swarthy one walked back to the chopper.

Hamil rested on the ground, a patch of purple wild flowers called "squaw's carpet" against his face, hearing a bee's timeless buzz nearby, and farther away a cricket—in resignation, able to muster only the barest contempt for his captors, and even that devoid of anger.

"Moccasins, eh?" the red head exclaimed. "You Indian?"

To which Hamil merely grunted.

Then after a moment's silence, questions again. "What made you do it anyway? Who put you up to it?"

Hamil raised up awkwardly on one side, spitting a piece of grass from between his lips and showing a faint spark. "Do you think it had to be somebody put me up to it?" he said. "Your people put me up to it and what they've done to the Lake."

"What about Glenbrook? Did you do Glenbrook, too?" The voice was young sounding and excited, on the edge of discovery.

"Detcord for Glenbrook, mines for the boat," Hamil said for no particular reason, his voice flat again and almost militarily matter of fact.

In the helicopter, orders were repeated over the static breakup, then Swarthy came back, the dead eyes in his mask face even blacker in anticipation. He couldn't stand these hippies anyway, and this one in particular. He'd had a couple of nice parties on the "Tahoe Dixie" and the bosses had treated him and the others to a whole night on the boat one time with the company whores.

"Hey," the red head greeted him, "he says he did Glenbrook, too!"

"Oh yeah, well our orders are to lean on him," was the dark leader's expressionless reply. He took a step forward suddenly and with heavy black boot kicked Hamil squarely in the face, changing his nose instantly to a mis-shapened, bleeding mass.

"Who put you up to it?" Hamil heard the guttural voice from what seemed like farther away.

"Your people," he said.

And again the boot, this time breaking his ribs, then twice in the kidneys as he tried to roll away.

"What do ya mean, my people?" the voice shouted, suddenly suspicious.

"He said because of what they've done to the Lake," red head clarified quickly.

"That right, hippie, you don't like what they've done to the Lake, so you start blowin' things up?" Hamil took another savage stomping of his kidneys.

"No, the clubs," Hamil gasped, an idea coming to him through the red fog and pain.

"What about the clubs?"

"Insurance, they wanted to collect insurance."

"That's not what he said before!" The red head whined defensively.

"He wasn't beat up before," Swarthy retorted sharply. Then he straightened up and, curiously, for a moment looked away— perhaps for the instant not even aware of the meadow or forest or freshening breeze, but in his mind's eye seeing something beyond.

"So now they're double crossin' you, is that what you're sayin'?" he said finally.

Hamil groaned, not sure he had the strength or the will.

"How much were they gonna pay you?"

"Fifty."

"Fifty thousand! And they're payin' us wages to snuff you."

Again Swarthy turned away and walked with firm strides back to the helicopter where a louder conversation ensued. Then, when he returned, he was carrying the M-16 again, but was still and would be always with Hamil's implanted doubt.

Again he kicked Hamil in the face, breaking his teeth.

"Who put you up to it?"

"The clubs," Hamil said, spitting out blood and broken pieces, determined now to hold to the idea.

"Who in the clubs?"

"I don't know. They didn't give names."

Again the foot in his broken ribs.

"Where'd you get the explosives?"

"The same guys." He gasped unable to breathe.

Swarthy stepped aside one last time. "I don't know if this guy's lyin' or not," he said to Red, his lowered voice still audible to Hamil on the ground. "On the radio, they say they never heard of him."

Suddenly, frustrated, he turned back. "Hippie, this is it. Either you tell me now or it's lights out. Who gave you the detcord?" He stood, scowling down at Hamil, gripping the rifle in both hands.

And Jeff Hamil, lying on his side now, bleeding and mangled, but with his head again raised above the sod, managed once more. "The clubs," he said, feeling somewhere inside himself a grim, wry satisfaction.

Strangely too, as he lay there, he suddenly imagined he saw Ned and Tony and Indian Joe. They were standing with their hands up, as if the gun were being pointed at them, with Ned in the middle and Tony and Joe on either side. Still, they stood strong and seemingly unafraid, and seeing them like that, gave him a sudden surge of hope—hope which oddly he now understood.

"Oh, Jesus!" he said, trying to focus more closely on Ned; and at once an unaccountable peace settled over him. He looked into the gun barrel uncomprehendingly then, like a wounded doe— just before the bullet slammed into his brain.

Afterwards, when the young pilot wondered about burying him, Swarthy declined. In fact, as they approached, and for no apparent reason, he plunged the bayonet savagely into Hamil's side.

"Why'd you do that?" the red haired man asked, getting perhaps a more complete insight into his companion. "He was already dead."

The other shrugged. "Just drag him over in the rocks," he said. And then, with not even a trace of his usual satisfied smile, "even if somebody finds him, it won't really matter."

PART II: TONY

Chapter Ten

We rode for five hours in the darkness, not fast, just steadily, Indian Joe always up ahead with me following anxiously after his horse's light colored tail and Jeff behind me—up and down rocky mountain trails, thru a labyrinth of interconnected canyons, and then finally across gentler, sage covered hills— inhaling the smells of the West, sage and pine carried in the warm wind; then shivering as the air changed towards morning— moving, too, thru layers of sound: from vast pregnant silences, thru crickets' rising intensity, to owls' ghostly hooting, and coyotes' insane yowling—to arrive finally at four a.m. overlooking a poor Reno outskirts community known as Sun Valley.

Then, it was strange to see the glow of street lights after having camped on reservation lands without electric; and, as I sat astride my horse looking down on the little village of run down houses and trailers, I experienced a strong dose of what, I suppose, was "cultural shock."

When I first learned of my brother's death, I'd just landed my battered old crab boat at the fish dock near the Aleutian village where I live, bringing her safety thru the narrow rock jetties into the inner harbor. It was low tide and the legs on the pier stood tall and ungainly, climbing up out of the water towards the shore. It was not a favorable time for offloading because of the distance from the boat up to the dock, but it was the penalty we had to pay in order to get in safely ahead of the latest advancing storm.

The sky was slate gray and my two crew members on deck blew plumes of white steam with every breath exhaled. "Man, it's

71

getting cold!" one of them muttered as he made the spring line fast to the forward cleat, and as I came off the bridge onto the deck to see that all the lines were secure.

We had about five thousand pounds of crab live in the wells and the young Russian boys in their colorful woolens already were pushing white transfer tanks noisily out the dock towards us. Prentice, the be-spectacled Englishman, who ran the fish-house for our Japanese *overlords*, came out of the green painted building at the shore-side end as well—wearing white coveralls and typically hurrying, anxious to know just what we'd caught.

I looked up at him in the best tradition of fish boat captains—stern, fierce and implacable. Which goes with the territory and is a reflection of the hard work and generally incomprehensible dangers we face. Besides which, being in Alaska for a few years, fishing and fighting and drinking with the Russians—but mostly fighting—had changed me in some profound ways. Instead of the hundred and ninety pound stripling I'd been on arrival, I'd metamorphosed; and, at two hundred and forty pounds, I was treated now with a deference among the Russians tinged with fear. Now, they called me "The Bear." But the first years of scraping and scuffling were filled with vile names and meanness—which had tested and tempered me forever.

"Good trip, Bear?" the Englishman asked, his apple red cheeks glowing in contrast to his billowing white breath; and his blue eyes seeming even warm and friendly behind his gold rimmed spectacles.

"About five thousand," I grunted. And then it was that he handed me down a battered, dog-eared envelope.

"This came for you," he said, "and from all the various postmarks, it must have gone to all the islands in the chain before it got here."

I reached up and took it from him, glancing at it first merely with curiosity, noting it was simply addressed to:

Tony Hamil
Fish Houses
Aleutian Islands, Alaska

Which explained why it had been passed on from one cooperating postal clerk to another. But then too, I was struck in rapid succession with perplexity and anxiety, as I more closely regarded the shaky scrawl. Then something clicked in my mind, as I remembered from long ago and recognized it as belonging to my *uncle*, Indian Joe—arguing with myself immediately that it couldn't possibly be, then turning away from Prentice and going blindly back into the cabin to read and understand.

Indian Joe had been committed to a hospital for the criminally insane six years before, when he'd tried to blow up a white man's dam that had doomed the Lahontan cutthroat trout run in Nevada and hence the Indians' great fishery. And to the best of my knowledge, no one had heard from him ever since. My father, Ned, had exhausted every legal means to have him released, but to no avail. He wasn't allowed visitors—having been deemed (as part of the vendetta against my father) as too incorrigible; he never wrote to anyone; and finally was assumed by our family to be drugged and/or lobotomized—i.e., *dead.*

I turned on the light over the chart table and tore the end off the envelope, anxious and knowing somewhere within myself, I suppose, that the letter represented not only a threat for having penetrated my isolated existence, but also something more profound. I hadn't thought much about Joe for a long, long time and, to tell the truth, hadn't for years considered the possibility of his still existing. Yet, when I was growing up, of all people, Joe was the one to whom I'd been closest.

He'd been more to me than an uncle, or a brother, and even more to me than my father. He'd meant the outdoors to me; and knowledge of the wind and weather; and hunting trips, and camping under the stars; and fish knowledge which I still used, even in Alaska; and folk lore; and Indian medicine; and an ethical, if not spiritual, compass.

My heart pounded, as I drew the single, scribbled sheet out of the envelope.

"Tony," it said in even shakier scrawl, *"I think they got Jeff. I had a dream. I think he's dead. Come!"*

And, in that instant, my life was forever changed. I went below and sat on the edge of my bunk with my hands pressed to my head, stunned and with my breath taken away. I had no idea how he'd been able to get the letter out of the hospital and was dumbfounded that he'd thought to send it to the Aleutians; then remembered once he'd shown me an article about commercial fishing in the Aleutians—which in retrospect had influenced me in choosing a destination after my escape from Nevada, but to which at the time I'd given little apparent attention. But then, he'd always understood so much about which others had no inkling. And for that matter, if he dreamt that my brother, Jeff, was dead, then I had very little doubt that he was. In fact, even news of Jeff's being killed outright wouldn't have come as a particular shock, as ever since I'd left Nevada I'd known that worry and fear. The fact that the mobsters there had tolerated the antics of my crusading father for as long as they had—and without retaliating against his family—seemed always improbable in the extreme.

However, that Joe was alive and still a rational, functioning human being after six years of wrongful imprisonment in a *crazy house*—still thinking and still "dreaming" about my family—was just too much! And suddenly nothing else could take priority. Not my wife, the Aleut, or our baby son, or our house, or the boat or fishing. I was going to have to go back to Nevada; and, in my mind, in my existence, in my very perception of life and myself, there could be no other choice. Never mind that I was already wanted in Nevada, and that I might very well be called upon to commit other desperate acts once I got there. And never mind the fact that my chances for a long, peaceful and prosperous future would be incrementally diminished as well.

Presently, with a terrible old fire beginning to stir, I went back out on the deck where my two crew members were already unloading the crab; and I didn't even see them. I crossed to the rail, then climbed up the wood rung ladder to the top of the dock, and stumbled obliviously in towards the fish house and a talk with Prentice. I'd be leaving soon, I knew that, and arrangements would have to be made for someone else to run the boat.

Chapter Eleven

Once Indian Joe took Jeff and me on a climb up a rocky winding trail to the top of a mesa overlooking a far flung barren valley. There were no trees, just miles of gray-green sagebrush, clumped up rocks and distant hills and mountains which looked blue and purple under the partially clouded sky.

Joe had a .22 rifle and he lay a bullet down on a large boulder, then with Jeff and me at his side walked off fifty paces. He had us hide down behind some rocks—"in case of ricochet," he said—then lay down himself on another boulder nearby. Jeff and I peaked to see him aiming the rifle towards the other rock and the bullet which appeared tiny from where we were, and then I realized he was trying to "fire" the bullet on the rock with the slug from his rifle. He didn't look at us, but he must have felt us watching him, or maybe it was just that he knew boys.

"Heads down!" he snapped and a few seconds after we did as he said, he fired, the first report followed instantaneously by the second.

Jeff and I both jumped up to see and sure enough the bullet off the rock was gone and we both were cheering, causing Joe to smile faintly.

"I want you to shoot like that," he said seriously.

Jeff was eight then and I was twelve; and, after years of his not always patient training, we did.

By the time I landed in Nevada, a week after getting Joe's letter, fishermen on the dock might have had to look twice to recognize me, though I wasn't sure. The Aleut had helped me to dye my hair and beard snow white; I had some rimless little reading glasses to wear out towards the end of my nose; and I was sporting a three piece tweed suit with matching golf cap which I bought in the layover in Seattle. All of which taken together gave me the look of some larger than life writer of fiction, or perhaps an eccentric college professor.

My wife—lest I go on any farther without explaining—is like other Indians I've known, in that she has reduced life down, or perhaps in her case I should say she's *re-reduced* life down to the basics. You see, she was one of those rare Aleuts who *made it*— went to the University of Alaska in Fairbanks on a scholarship and excelled in a business curriculum—then worked for a big firm in Anchorage for a couple of years before returning to the Aleutians and home. And now she never speaks of the university or the business world or much of anything outside. But instead studies the old ways and, apart from Joe, I've learned the most from her— about the plants and trees and birds and weather—how to make things creatively from things with which we're already provided. And how, first and foremost, to exult in the absolute wonder of our own lives—to appreciate and actually love the doing of small survival tasks as a kind of exclamation point to the joy. It is so basic and yet missed by so many, who in their headlong quest for grander things miss the grandest thing of all, which is just to celebrate our lives.

Anyway my wife, whose Aleut name translates roughly into something like "the chuckling sound of two waters coming together," took the news of my departure with great, though un-protesting, concern. Which of course was also the way of her people, and had the effect of making me love her more—making it more difficult for me to leave. If we'd have had some knockdown, drag out fight over it, anger would have carried me easily to the airport and beyond; but as it was, I held her and our baby son, Joseph, alternately, and sometimes together, right up until the flight. And strangely, we talked about it almost not at all after my first terse announcement. Then the last day, we were nearly completely silent about everything, simply being in each others presence, intimately, and without a word—an Indian technique in times of trial which can *speak* with immense volume.

I took ten thousand dollars in cash out of one of our bank accounts before I left. I've done very well fishing in Alaska, especially the last two years since I've had the boat and, while ten thousand in cash may seem a lot of money, it represented my take of just a couple of good trips on the crab grounds. Anyway, I took the money with me, not knowing what I'd need or run into. Which brings up another good point about my Indian wife and which, I think, has involved a concentrated effort on her part, as not all of her people are this way. She simply doesn't care about money. She cares that we have basic things for our son, and that our house is warm and dry, and that we have food to eat. But as far as I know, she's never even wanted to know how much money we've had in the bank. Somehow, whatever the amount, it always has been assumed to be enough, and so hasn't mattered to her—which, increasingly, is how I've become myself.

Anyway, I took the money with me in cash, so as not to have to rely on traveler's checks and a fake ID to get them cashed. But I also did have a fake ID—an Alaskan driver's license concocted by Martin Wainwright, the engraver. Martin was once in the counterfeiting business in the *lower forty-eight*—until the Feds made it too hot for him and he found it necessary to start a new career with the rest of us fugitives in the far North. Still, the fires of rebellion burn on within him and drive his somewhat perverse creativity—so that my driver's license was an inevitable Wainwright masterpiece, complete with my new white haired and white bearded picture, and with the authentic serial numbers off the license of a local fisherman named Martin Sikorsky who was presumed recently drowned, but whose body was as yet unfound.

How Martin Wainwright had managed to get Martin Sikorsky's driver's license number was beyond me, and I didn't ask. In Alaska, it's not considered good form to pry too deeply into another man's business, especially since a lot of business conducted there is—like Martin Wainwright's—a bit on the shady side. So that I merely paid Martin Wainwright's fee and accepted the card, grateful for professional results, however they were obtained.

I got on the plane *as Martin Sikorsky* with some confidence regarding my disguise and the ID, but then on the flight down to

Seattle and during the layover and throughout the flight onto Reno had too much time to think and worry.

Actually, it started out with more thinking about Joe. Once the plane was airborne and the seat belt sign had been turned off and the other obligatory procedures had been run through—i.e., the serving of complimentary drinks and peanuts; the renting of earphones; and advertising via the movie screen of duty free merchandise, etc., etc., ad nauseam—I took Joe's letter out and re-read it for about the twentieth time. I was seated by myself towards the rear and, as the plane was fortunately not crowded, was able to drape my oversize body over seats rather than over other people.

I still couldn't understand how Joe had known where to send the letter, and even wondered if somehow he'd finally managed to escape from the hospital. On occasion over the years, I'd had letters from Nevada—from my Aunt Marguerite and less frequently from Jeff before he'd gone off to Viet Nam—but they'd never mentioned anything about Joe except for one time I remember Jeff speculating that Joe must have died or been turned into a vegetable zombie since such a long time had passed, and there'd been no news of any attempted escape. Jeff said he'd called the hospital, too, a couple of times, inquiring after Joe's well being; but each time the terse response was the same—that there was *no information available on that particular prisoner at that particular time*. So that then, Jeff had concluded, since there never was any communication from Joe himself, it must be that he *couldn't* communicate anymore. And it made me sick that I'd bought into it—taken the easy way out, accepted it, and just quit thinking about him as being alive.

Indians, I've noticed, often seem to have a different concept of time from our own—rather a flowing along instead of our continual fighting upstream (for deadlines' sake). Which generates an equanimity and aura of timelessness that seems to translate directly to the capacity to endure. I knew that and certainly should have known that's how it would be with Joe, an Indian's man's man above all else.

A white man, for example, would think it impossible and even insane to go for years without saying something, while I could see Joe doing exactly that, if he thought it were necessary, or even if he thought there wasn't anything particular to say.

And anyway, the longer I sat in that airplane seat, contemplating Joe's letter, and Joe, the more it grew on me—that Joe still *was* a live and functioning human being, with beating heart and, most especially, with functioning brain—in amongst the crazy people. And it scalded my conscience with shame, not so much because we hadn't figured out a way to get Joe out, as that had always seemed impossible after my father Ned's efforts had failed, and given our family's bent towards the law and doing things *legally*. But scalded because I'd simply stopped thinking about him, and because I'd gone along and gotten on with my own life—for *six long years*—while Joe in silence had endured. Still thinking about us.

"I think Jeff's dead," his letter said.

Dreaming about us. "I had a dream."

Finally, I wept on the plane—something I don't ever recall doing as an adult—and, when I did, I made a vow to myself thru clenched teeth that I was going to get Joe out of that prison—*whatever it took*.

The day went on and that first flight ended and melted into the layover in Seattle, and then into the onward flight. And my thoughts moved, too, from Joe; to what might be done; and to the immediate dangers ahead.

Since I'd slugged and broken the jaw of the mobster's favorite shill newspaper editor the last time I was there (and, given the long standing enmity they had for Ned and our family besides), they'd like nothing better than to lock me away as well. Then, if they'd actually gotten Jeff, as Joe dreamed, their victory would be complete. Ned and Jeff both dead, me in jail and Joe in the crazy house. And, so much for the Hamil legacy.

Then my nervousness began to grow and I started second guessing myself, in spite of my resolve.

'How exactly did I expect to go about things? Where would I start? Should I try to see Joe? And how could I do that, either as Tony Hamil or Martin Sikorsky? One being wanted and the other unknown.'

'And what about Jeff? Should I try to find him first? And what if he were dead? What could I do if he were? Wage a one man (assuredly to the death) war against the Mob, who ran everything there?'

None of it really made sense at that point, and in fact seemed less and less logical as each passing minute brought me closer to it. Indian Joe's letter had said "come!" though and, logic or not, I was doing just that. And for the rest, I knew I had to be extremely wary and see.

Finally on the ground at the Reno Airport, I moved off towards the baggage claim area, feeling at once strangely out of place and, as if I'd traveled back thru time and not just over distance. So much had happened since I'd been there that essentially I was a different person; and yet inevitably, there were stirrings of the old Tony Hamil down inside me. Once familiar sights were still there—the rows of slot machines in the airport lobby, for example. And I was assailed by unexpected lonely and strangely uncomfortable feelings—which bordered on the perverse wish that I hadn't left in the first place, and thus hadn't *missed* all that had taken place.

Later, after getting my bag, I took a cab to Aunt Marguerite's house in the suburbs where, if anything, the discomfort of feeling myself in a time warp intensified. I opened Marguerite's white picket gate and then was assaulted by an absolute flood of memories, for where Marguerite lived was where my grandparents had lived; and my mother until she'd gotten married; and other aunts and uncles; and Indian Joe.

I knocked on the door, feeling as if I were going to hyperventilate; and then I could hear her coming on her metal crutches—struck down with polio in her twenties, a lovely young woman sentenced then to a lifetime of wishing for what could have been.

She opened the door and then, once again, I had to have doubts about my disguise. For almost immediately, she was in my arms, her hot tears against my neck.

"Oh Tony!" she said, "Oh Tony, it's been so long!"

And afterwards, we went inside and had tea at the dark old dining room table, which was another link to my childhood and the past.

Chapter Twelve

I haven't meant to create the impression that I didn't care about my brother, Jeff. Like most brothers, Jeff and I had our differences and, while I continued to hold him in high regard, my conversation with Aunt Marguerite brought those problems back anew.

As in the chemistry of all families, there were personality quirks in each of us which, when stirred into the family pot, either mixed, combined or clashed—often depending upon the presence or absence of other family members at particular times and places. And while I think no one is ever *totally* successful in sorting out the whats and whys of feelings engendered by family doings, and held by family members one for the other, to this day I don't understand much of our situation at all. Just that it was complex, especially with the Indians thrown into the equation; and meetings like the one I had with Aunt Marguerite always caused me to re-examine in detail—always working towards some hoped for peace of mind.

I was older than Jeff by four years, but never really set the kind of example for him which our parents desired. I was not good in school, didn't care about it, and wasn't particularly polite either. What I liked was the outdoors and I lived for outings with Indian Joe. And while Jeff shared these outings when we were young, later as a teenager, he gravitated more towards Ned, often staying back talking politics, or indulging in some of his other interests.

And ultimately, it was ok with me. In fact, I took great pride in a statement Joe once made about us: 'that Jeff was like an Indian, but that Tony really was one.' And I took pride in it, not only because Joe, the authority, said it, but also because it just felt

82

good to be rated ahead of Jeff in anything. Jeff, after all, was the *gifted one*—the artist and pianist whom my mother doted upon, the good student and athlete who could always be depended upon to be *responsible.*

And it was especially galling because he was younger, yet it was he who apparently was setting the example. In earlier times, we would compete and rivalries would end often in fist fights, which I would win because of my size and age advantage, but which I ultimately would lose, also, because of our mother's sympathy for Jeff, which I construed as favoritism. And later on, while we didn't fight anymore, when we did things in the outdoors without Joe, we often went our separate ways—Jeff and his friends preferring the environs around Lake Tahoe, while I fished and hunted and camped along the river.

In the beginning, when Jeff began getting so interested in the politics of the area, and asking our dad, Ned, all kinds of questions, I thought it was some sort of put on, or maybe "a cottoning up," as Ned would have termed it. But then, as it continued to where it dominated our dinner conversations, and almost all of our other family time together, I felt increasingly betrayed. Ned would rant and rave about the gamblers and what they'd done and were doing to our environment, and Jeff would voice observations which I guess Ned thought were pretty smart because they'd fire him up some more. And my Mom, who I'm sure would have paid money to just one time hear something positive about her native State of Nevada, would join me in being silent. I didn't really care about the gamblers and what they were doing; at that point, there seemed to be plenty of country and water to go around. And all I could really focus on was the next big trout I was going to catch, or the next buck or bear Joe and I might track. And underneath that were the pure harmonious thoughts that being one with nature were teaching me.

At length I did get involved, though; and in retrospect, and to be honest, I suppose it was at least partially out of envy of Jeff and of trying to be recognized by my dad. What a mistake! In fact, after years in Alaska, I guess I'd become pretty hard bitten because when I thought of all the idealistic ideas Ned and Jeff shared, I got sick to my stomach. You know like, *one man can make a difference* and *if a man tries hard enough, justice will prevail.* And, what did any of that ever get Ned? Except bleeding ulcers and a lot of dangerous enemies, plus a cruelly unfair press which brought pain even to his relationship with his family. It would have been far better, I thought, just to pick up and move on, instead of pining after some *pie in the sky* democracy there.

The only expression I ever heard that remotely fit the Nevada *legal system* was that, *when the fix is equal, justice will prevail*—but even that didn't quite get the essence of it, if the question considered involved mob interests versus people interests. Then, of course, if dissenters thought that justice might be achieved thru some sort of equality in bribery, they would find out very quickly instead that in Nevada there could be only one side in such cases. And ultimate *justice* came when necessary out of the barrels of mobsters' guns. Bleached bones scattered in the surrounding desert spoke of those who'd found that out the hard way.

But as I say, this one time I did get involved. I'd just gotten out of the Army and, much like Jeff would do later on, I'd re-enrolled at the university, hoping to finish my degree. One day though, not long after getting back, I went for a bike ride out along the river to a place called Mayberries, where Jeff and I and Indian Joe, and sometimes even Ned, liked to fish in the spring. There was an old sawmill there and an ancient, rickety wooden bridge. And on that particular afternoon, there were many memories amidst the wafting smells of the raw lumber—of cool misty mornings together there along the bank, and plump trout gleaming silver and cold to the touch.

But something else, too—and I'll never forget it—I noticed after awhile a huge, just placed black on white billboard sign announcing that the fields there bordering the river were to be the site for Reno's coming "New Industrial Park."

And after staring at it for awhile, I guess you could say I came unhinged. At least I reacted in a way I never had before (or since). I became an activist.

It just didn't make sense to me to put industry of any kind on that river, while in every direction there were thousands of square miles of open rangeland which would have served every bit as well. Besides, I liked Mayberries just as it had always been; I still had a chip on my shoulder from being in the Army; and I found the very term itself "industrial park" offensive in the extreme and an affront to anybody's intelligence.

So that anyway, to make a long story short, I joined with some of my old beer drinking buddies, and we got up a petition to change the zoning so that they couldn't put the thing there—or, to be completely accurate, we got the idea for the petition and Ned drew it up for us. Then afterwards, all kinds of volunteers joined up to circulate it—friends of the beer drinkers and university people and others.

To understand, too, as to why it turned into a *cause celebre* among the artsy-craftsy folk at the college, a person needs to know more about the river itself. The Truckee was at that point still a clear brilliant mountain stream—at least the upper thirty or forty miles of it, dropping down from the pine wooded Sierra range at Lake Tahoe to cut its way thru forbidding black rock canyons inland, to water the Truckee meadows wherein lay Reno, and then flow on afterwards across sage dotted, arid country to Pyramid Lake Pyramid, itself a semi-alkaline remnant of a once great inland sea, from which the extraordinary strain of giant cutthroat trout had made annual spawning migrations back up the river to Tahoe and *its* tributaries—the total ecosystem a remarkable, land locked, mirror image in miniature of the great salmon spawning systems of the North Pacific.

The white men had ruined the lower river, though, with their dams and irrigation projects, and doomed the great fish run even before I was born. Still upstream—above Reno, where Mayberries was, and beyond—the river descended in a series of rapids, falls and deep swirling pools, where lesser trout—rainbows and browns—schooled thickly and grew themselves to impressive size.

So that with the pollution of Tahoe already well under way and Pyramid Lake at the other end drying up as a result of the irrigating, and the lower river a dammed up and corrupted mess, this so-called "park" at Mayberries represented more than just the ruination of Mayberries itself, but was the first major encroachment on the upper river—which was all that was left.

And, the more I thought about the whole thing, the crazier I became—for awhile even crazier than my father and brother had been all along.

I started off by writing letters to the newspaper editor—even before the petition—and got others to do the same, until finally we were excoriated by the editor in reply. At which point, I went door to door with the petition, and made speeches to environmental groups and women's groups, and went on TV to be mocked and ridiculed by the media puppets. And stirred up the liberals on campus to a feeding frenzy.

Jeff, who wasn't even eighteen at the time, got some of his high school friends to help him put flyers on windshields in shopping center parking lots, and to distribute bumper stickers, also—all of which were funded out of my own meager savings and the contributions of other "crazies". And then finally, and best of all, we were joined in full force by my father, Ned—who, as the list of names on the petition reached into the thousands, scheduled the necessary hearings and represented us before the County Commissioners.

It was a real happening! There were signs in store windows and on cars all over town carrying the urgent message to "save the river"; and huge crowds of supporters turned out and jammed the Commission chambers for three consecutive days and nights of hearings. Ned made wonderful, fiery speeches, quoted routinely out of context, of course, by the prostitute press. The evening editor wrote scathing editorials calling Ned a "populist"—a euphemism in this case for "communist"—saying Ned, 'was seeking to dictate the use of private lands.'

Still, an impressive number of other advocates for the zone change gave vent to their feelings before the Commission, as well. I was introduced as the originator of the petition and, also, got to speak. And two attorneys for the land developers spoke, briefly, also.

Then, after the three days and nights of haranguing, when it came down to a final vote, of course we lost. Two of the five commissioners voted in our favor—in favor of the zone change; two voted against; and the Chairman, whom my dad always regarded as a fair man, and one who wouldn't take a bribe, broke the tie by voting against.

"If it comes down to a tie and the Chairman has to break it," I remember Ned saying, "we'll be in good hands. Old Ray's a fisherman. He grew up around here and understands, not like these Johnny Come Latelies."

Yeah, right! And Nevada really is a State in the American Union!

I remember afterwards sitting for a long time side by side with my dad in that emptied out meeting hall—and with Jeff on his other side—in silence, almost like in church, and without looking up. And I knew deep down inside me that something had gone out of Ned forever. It was kind of as if he'd shrunk up within himself, as he realized this time they'd not just beaten him, but had made a mockery of the very principles of democracy and justice he'd raised us on—but, with us as victims, too, this time, and not merely as lookers on.

I remember thinking as we sat there in stunned silence, how it had been a long time since he'd come there from the old South— a long time since he'd fallen in love with our wild, lovely western country and tried to convey that passion to those who'd grown up there—who returned his enthusiasm with an inexplicable boredom, which bordered on contempt.

Thinking about that really tore me up most of all and, still young, I reached an arm across his shoulders, choking back a sob as I did so. Then, that night made the near fatal mistake of going by myself unthinkingly into a downtown bar, not far from the newspaper building. I just wanted to be alone, have a beer and forget about the whole thing, and didn't even consider what part of town I was in.

I walked inside and it was dim-lit and rather elegant, I remember, with lots of dark wood paneling and mirrors. A couple of groups were sitting at tables off to the side, but there wasn't anyone at the bar. And I was glad, wanting, as I said, just to be by myself. But then almost right away, a voice cut thru the place like a buzz saw and, squinting again into the gloom, I too late recognized the night editor who'd alluded to Ned, and all of us really, as being communists.

"Hey, young Hamil, kind of left you neutered today, didn't we boy?" he called out in his braying loud voice, and with his cronies around him laughing and smirking and nudging each other. "In fact," he went on, "it was more like we made you over into women, didn't we?"

And right away I felt my cheeks flush with anger and embarrassment. "We?" I said, trying to fight back but not very loudly, "I thought you were the impartial media."

He chuckled and, standing up from his table, swayed towards me, big and flabby with a paunch, and with very mean eyes set in a florid, horsy face.

"We can have you Hamil's for breakfast, don't you understand that?" he said brimming with overconfidence. "In fact, we can have you anytime we want you."

"We?" I repeated, this time a little more strongly. "You mean you're not much of anything yourself—not without your gangster cronies?"

He smiled his mean smile again and then reached out and pushed me hard in the chest, knowing full well what he was doing—drawing a hot headed young guy straight into trouble.

In that, he succeeded, too, though I'm sure he didn't foresee such a drastic result for himself.

Typically, I struck without thinking, forgetting the Indian discipline Joe had always sought to instill—forgetting to strike only when the odds were in my favor, or, at the very worst, when they were even. Reacting to the push reflexively and out of anger, I crossed my right over his extended arm and I got all of him. The tremendous impact on his jaw sent a shock wave clear up into my shoulder; and he went down like a sack of cement.

Then, immediately, I had to fight my way in sheer desperation out of the place. Three or four of his friends jumped up and tried to get a hold of me; and I swung and swung again like a wild man, then twisted and jerked and finally broke free. I burst thru the door and hit the street running, knowing full well right then that, if I were caught, I was as good as in prison. Because in that town, then as now, there is (as I've said) only one side to every story—their side. And my argument that the editor had instigated the fight by pushing me first would be simply a non-argument—

since everyone in that bar, bartender included and probably leading the pack, would testify routinely that I marched in there and landed a totally unprovoked blow.

I ran, hitchhiked, stowed away in a semi, rode in a boxcar across Canada, and finally got to fly the last leg to sanctuary in the islands of the far North. Leaving Ned and my brother to face the embarrassing headlines, not to mention Gestapo style questioning as to my whereabouts—questions which I made sure they couldn't answer by not communicating with them, or anybody, for a very long time.

Chapter Thirteen

Marguerite said Jeff had a girl friend who worked in the University library, and whose name was Sue Marie. And the very fact that Marguerite knew her name was revolutionary because my brother Jeff was always shy about such matters and *never* confided them in anyone.

"He actually talked about her," Marguerite said, a soft chuckle emanating from somewhere within her wizened up little frame. "And he promised to bring her around for a visit, but he never has," she added—noting also that the last time she'd seen Jeff, which was about a month before, he'd seemed despondent and pre-occupied and, though she hadn't asked, she'd assumed things weren't going as well.

Marguerite filled me in, also, on various news from the many scattered aunts, uncles and cousins; and, somewhere in the midst of it, there was talk of Lake Tahoe and news of the explosions at Glenbrook and the sinking of the tour boat. But there was no connection at that point, just the usual assumptions about some sort of gangland happenings.

To tell the truth, too, the interlude with her in the old house had the effect of lulling me—of making me forget I was a fugitive and of taking me back in time, when there was no danger; and because of her relatively recent dealings with Jeff and her conversations reflecting it, I found myself believing that maybe things were all right after all, and that maybe Jeff really was alive.

I was so comfortable, in fact, that I didn't start to worry afresh until after I'd again anonymously telephoned the rooming house where Jeff had been living, and was told by the landlady that she *still* hadn't seen him and would appreciate getting the rent.

Then, when Aunt Marguerite suggested she'd give me a ride in her old car to the university, to try to speak with Jeff's girl friend, it came back to me full force—that I still *was* a fugitive and was already putting Marguerite at some risk.

So that I hugged her then and assured her that I'd be back, but that I thought it best to be cautious. Then leaving my suitcase with every intention of returning, I nevertheless took the briefcase with the money as a hedge if I couldn't, and walked the few blocks to the city bus stop.

I rode the bus across the city, nervous but still taking notice of Reno's new skyline, amazed by the proliferation of tall new hotels and wondering what schemes were afoot to provide adequate water in that mostly arid high desert. The river was small and insignificant in the face of the burgeoning tourist population, and it was easy to imagine some devious plan afoot for draining *ex-national treasure* Lake Tahoe down in slow increments until finally it was a mere shadow remnant like the Indian Reservation's Pyramid Lake. And of course by the time that was finished, the perpetrators would be dead from old age, or overindulgence, and then it wouldn't be their concern.

I got off the bus at the university, feeling very much alone and not a little bit afraid. I walked across the inner quad, which was a great grassy rectangular expanse, surrounded by trees and old buildings, and with the modern brick and glass library up at one of the far corners. And I was lucky because it was a Friday afternoon and there weren't many people about; still I was uneasy because six years before, and because of the petition drive, I'd known, not just a lot of students (who'd be gone or graduated by now), but also a lot of the professors as well.

I walked fast along the sidewalks, carrying the briefcase and looking straight ahead, of course not wanting to recognize anyone, nor in anyway to call attention to myself. Still with every step, I imagined myself being scrutinized and expected at any moment for some challenge to come, thinking again if someone spoke to me, I'd answer only in Russian and pretend not to understand.

But then those fears proved groundless, as I didn't encounter anyone; then, after what seemed a very long time, I reached the library and mounted the few steps to the swinging glass doors.

I took a deep breath and glanced briefly back across the quad where I'd come from, then pushed the door and entered the hushed world inside, thinking to sit down somewhere as soon as possible and so draw the minimum attention to myself, believing that after I'd been absorbed into the scene for awhile, then I could move about quietly within the quietness and notice without being noticed.

Still, I had to cross the entrance lobby and pass by the horseshoe shaped front desk where several girls were working. And while I ignored the temptation to look at them right then and perhaps spot Jeff's friend, still I felt their eyes following me until I'd passed into the stacks, then on into the reference reading area. Doubtless noticing my size and white hair and wondering, however briefly, if I were a visiting professor or lecturer, or perhaps just a visitor from the local community.

There were only a couple of other people at the tables in the reference room, who of course also stared at the *giant* newcomer, adding to my self consciousness. But then fortuitously, I spotted stacked up back issues of the local newspapers on shelves in the corner; and, with that, I had a reason for being there. In the Aleutians, we're not privy to much news from the outside, getting only stale, little single sheet summaries which arrive irregularly on the twice weekly flights from Kodiak. So that I went happily over and scooped up an armload of the papers—notwithstanding the laughable Reno bias—and deposited them afterwards on the nearest vacant table.

Then I set about reading, still aware of my dangerous situation, but actually somewhat distracted by my sheer hunger for news—working backward from the present and, while essentially skipping national and international stories which I knew about, delving fascinated into the local.

I read about an ongoing scandal involving a local bordello owner who'd failed to pay his proper share of taxes to the IRS, and subsequently bribed a federal judge who'd also gotten caught— thinking to myself such a thing never would have come to light in

Nevada unless he, or the judge, or both, had gangland enemies higher up.

Then I read an editorial about a pollution study of Lake Tahoe being done by outside federal experts, whose techniques, results and generally unfavorable attitudes were typically called very much into question by the editor—my old *friend*. And, I read about casino profits being down, of course, so that in the coming year there'd be less tax money for schools; and another editorial about an apparently *unreasonable* request by the Pyramid Lake Indians for an increased flow of river water to the lake.

I read about another big new casino development being approved by the TRPA (Tahoe Regional Planning Agency) for Tahoe's South Shore, and almost laughed out loud at the terms used in the story: *careful consideration, prudent impact studies* and *environmentally sound planning*. Noticing also that nothing was said about how the voting had gone within the agency, knowing full well how it had gone anyway—just like it had always gone in such decisions over the years with the majority against the proposal but with the minority having their way because of the clever anomaly of *dual majority vote* insisted upon from the beginning by the *Nevada Legislature*.

And I read on about all the marquee attractions coming to the clubs—an endless cavalcade of big name stars, whose continued coming to the area made it *such a great place to live*.

Over an hour passed and, while I remained wary and watchful most of the time and with the primary mission of talking to the girl remaining uppermost in my mind, still the news stories did allow me to relax more than I would have expected. And while at intervals I tried to consider various strategies for approaching her—if she were there—and for talking to her without revealing my identity, I remained unable to get a clear picture of it and finally decided I'd simply have to be flexible and ad lib as the situation unfolded.

Then after awhile, my reading room companions departed, leaving me finally alone—which is how I was when I came face to face with a front page picture of the *Tahoe Dixie,* and a huge headline telling of her sinking—a spread which would have done justice to the beginning or ending of World War III.

According to the story, the explosion was assumed to have been caused by vapors in the bilge, and not the result of any act of sabotage. And while there had been no eyewitnesses, there was a night watchman who, nevertheless, also reported having seen no one.

I read and re-read it, thinking too after the second reading that the whole thing smelled like a rotten old fish. Because, in the first place, I was quite certain the boat had diesel engines rather than gas, so that there wouldn't have been explosive vapors in the bilge; and then too, if an act of sabotage wasn't suspected, why should it be brought up at all? And why even mention the night watchman, if he, too, were a non-witness?

Still, I shrugged it off with a disdain shaped over years of living with Ned, again thinking it was just the gangsters playing games, and basically ignoring a kind of faint, nagging uneasiness, which in fact at the time I barely noticed.

Then I decided it was time to be about my real business there. I stood up and went first into the restroom, which was nearby; then afterward, with my head down apparently in deep thought, moved on up alongside the front desk. I picked up a flyer from a piled up stack and, pretending to read, took the opportunity to survey the several girls working there. One tall blond down at the end was assisting a girl student checking out several books; another, a brunette with short hair and glasses, was seated at a small desk behind, bent over some paperwork. And then I saw the girl, Sue Marie.

She was working several paces up along the counter, dressed in dark slacks and crisp tan and white gingham, short sleeved blouse—busily checking in a pile of returned books, and close enough that I could get a clear look at her name tag. And it half panicked me, finding her so quickly, and still not knowing exactly what I was going to say.

I thought she was very attractive, without makeup but with a kind of glowing, healthy outdoor look. She was medium height, with medium length dark hair brushed glossy, and had smart brown eyes—seemingly very absorbed and coolly efficient, while systematically canceling the books into a computer, then placing them on a cart for re-distribution. Having, too, a certain softness of expression around her eyes and mouth which was probably attractive to Jeff, as it seemed to speak of understanding, compassion and sympathy—but which, as it turned out, went one typical step beyond, advertising a firm belief in Mom and apple pie all right, but, also, an absolutely blind faith in the righteousness and decency of local institutions.

Immediately though, she glanced over and asked if I needed help; and there was a kind of playful twinkle in her eyes, as if somehow she actually suspected my looking at the flyers was a kind of put on. So that then, I was even more wary, sensing she was nobody's fool.

I shook my head to her offer, and she continued her task with the books. Then after another minute of reading about a summer concert series—which was the topic of the pamphlet—I exited again to the other room and my newspapers, knowing now who she was, but still not knowing how it was all going to translate into knowledge of Jeff.

In retrospect it seems elementary, too; but in the midst of it, I was so afraid of being discovered that I was slow to see things clearly. To that point, I simply hadn't been able to figure out how to ask her about Jeff without revealing myself, and, back at the table when I finally did realize what I should have done—that I should have immediately acknowledged having heard of her, introduced myself as Martin Sikorsky, Jeff's friend from Alaska, and invited her to my table to talk—it was simply too late. That would have been up front and straightforward and certainly more believable than somehow, after the fact, trying now to go back in and engage her in a conversation, wherein I would pretend not to have heard of her, but somehow coincidentally lead her around to a discussion of Jeff anyway.

And as I recognized the blown opportunity, it was maddening, sickening, and at that point little consolation to remind myself I wasn't practiced in such matters, and not a quick study in them either. Because simply put, if I were going to survive, I'd better be getting things right the first time.

And then there was something else, too—something triggered by being back in that once familiar environment where other frustrations had ended bitterly. I stared at the newspapers again, but I wasn't seeing them, as the terrible hostility I have within me was rising up, fueled not just by the immediate failure, but by these other instances from my past. And I can honestly say that I probably never would have married the Aleut if it weren't for those earlier disappointments, so profound were their effects on me, and even in spite of being in exile in the far flung north where selection of female companions was limited.

Truth to tell, and in spite of my youthful involvement with Indian Joe and the Indians, I always had gone with white girls and always had seen myself as one day being married to one. But then after all that happened to me—and with the exception of true Christians, of whom I thought there were not many even in church—I finally had come to the point of not liking white American females at all, of not daring to like them. And now, having to play cat and mouse with Jeff's girl friend, who on the surface at least was striking, and whom I really wanted to like, was for me (especially in that campus context) a serious psychological twisting.

About my hostility, too: Once when I first went in the Army, I was subjected to a whole battery of psychological placement tests, and I was clear off the scale in the hostility area— something they said 'might give me problems later on in civilian life,' but which was apparently more than acceptable for their immediate purposes. But then that's a whole other story, and I only bring up my hostility here to illustrate a point. That is, in the presence of the Aleut it doesn't exist; and I think it goes back to our courtship days when I would present her with a bouquet of wildflowers, or just a single wildflower. And her enthusiasm and unrestrained joy were so spontaneous and genuine and without concern as to what messages they might or might not be sending, that I was totally disarmed —having grown up around the other in my own culture, which was diametrically opposite, selfish and always a fuel for anger.

I remember even in grade school little girls hanging around wanting to be my friend, I thought, but the minute I gave them a gift—a flower, or a lucky penny or some such—it was as if they lost interest entirely. They wouldn't talk to me anymore; I simply vanished from their screens—until later on, late in high school, when I finally got smart (or hurt badly enough) and did what my buddies had always told me to do.

"Treat'em like dirt and you won't be able to get rid of them," they'd said. And so I did, doing away with all signs of emotion or caring, never giving anybody anything; having a flip comment for every situation, no matter how serious; and, of course, concentrating ferociously on sports—in my case hunting and fishing and football. So that by the time I did go in the Army, there were three or four coeds literally fighting over me, and I don't know who disgusted me more, the girls or my own self for playing the game.

One woman I really did love, though—even after knowing how to play the game. I loved her before I went off to Alaska; loved her in college and while studying with her in that same library; and loved her while I was away in the service, too. But, I didn't want to lose her, of course, so I never dared to tell her I loved her (telling an American girl "I love you" being after all, I thought, the ultimate kiss good-bye).

So that I just played along slyly and took from her all she'd given me, then came home from the Army to find somebody else sleeping with her. And why not? 'There was no commitment was there?' She was extremely reasonable in explaining that to me— careful even, just in case I had "feelings" for her (whatever that meant)—patting my arm like the good nurse she was, though actually I felt more as if a surgeon had just carved another piece out of my humanity. And I wondered if I should ask her: 'should I go to the end of the line and just wait until her new friend had to go in the Army or somewhere, too, and whoever else there might be, as well. And then was it possible my number would come up again?' And, wasn't that what it was all about, anyway?— interchangeable parts.

And thinking about my brother, too, and his girl friend whom I'd just met, I couldn't say for sure that it would be more of the same and not an exception to the rule. But what I knew about Jeff was that, as often as he might have been rejected and hurt, he simply had too much integrity ever to give in and play along. And probably too, that's why he'd never talk about such things; there was just too much pain.

Chapter Fourteen

"European women are the true lovers," or so said a sergeant I knew in the military. He'd spent a couple of tours in Europe and had married a Finnish woman; and one night, when we were all having a few beers together, he came out with it.

"They always have time to smell a rose and they always take time to probe feelings—everybody's feelings. Because they understand feelings are the food and drink of what we are."

And, of course, all the guys got all over him.

"Yeah, Sarge, have another beer!"

"You're just trying to rationalize not marrying an American."

"No," he said, "I mean it. They take the trouble to love everybody—and I don't mean sexually—and everybody's better off for it, including the women. And that's what winds up making them the sexiest women in the world."

"Yeah, sure Sarge, and that's why you're out drinkin' with us and not home in bed."

I have to admit when he first said it, I didn't quite get it either, didn't quite know what he was talking about and pretty much went along with the general opinion that he was just another boozy sergeant, philosophizing to hear himself ('I was an American, after all, and wasn't everything American the best?'). Still, it stayed with me, partly I'm sure because of my different experience in having been close to the Indians. So that in fact, I did mull over what he'd said from time to time, until later on when another buddy—a Frenchman named Henri, who'd grown up in Tahiti—put it more succinctly, but in re-enforcing the other, helped me finally to understand.

"Island people," he said, "always take the time to love each other because they know pretty soon they'll all be dead."

And so it is with my Aleutian wife and her people, where hardship and danger are so close and not papered over with even thin veneer—where relationships are vital and clung to with fierceness, if not desperation; and where moments together with anyone are deemed precious and golden.

Unexpectedly, the girl came into the reading room then, interrupting my thought pattern disarmingly, and afterwards proceeding to do the very worst thing imaginable. She approached my table shyly, it seemed, now wearing a white cardigan over the tan blouse and against the air conditioned chill; then proceeded absolutely to blow me away.

"Excuse me," she said prettily, "but you looked so familiar to me out there. You aren't by some chance related to Jeff Hamil, are you?"

Her words hung there and I was sent reeling, not knowing what to do.

"What?" I choked, managing to buy time then with a sudden and prolonged coughing spasm.

"I'm sorry," I said finally, "I was really into these papers and didn't quite hear you."

"Oh, it's nothing," she said, in what had to rank as *the* great understatement in my life. "I was just wondering if you were related to a guy I know named Jeff Hamil?"

I stared at her across the table, fetchingly posed with both hands gripping the top of a chair back, leaning forward with her mouth pursed in sincerity and apparently serious interest. And, somewhere—I think at first in my subconscious—I recognized that this was already the most intimate situation I'd been in with an attractive white female since winding up in the Aleutians.

"You look so much like him across the eyes," she said, lifting a hand from the chair then and moving it back and forth across her own smart brown eyes, as if she were drawing a line.

And wary of certain distracting stirrings, I forced myself to focus, though still not knowing what to do. If I denied I was related and she went away, how would I be able to bring up the subject of Jeff to her again? And on the other hand, if I admitted I was related—that I was Jeff's brother—would she maybe turn me in? It would all depend upon what Jeff had told her, I knew; and also, on if—as Marguerite had surmised—she were mad at him, or they'd had a falling out—both of which were variables which I couldn't predict.

Finally though in desperation, and with the clock running down on my speechlessness, I hit on a middle course, still presenting myself as Martin Sikorsky, but pretending to know the Hamil's as well.

"Wow! What an amazing coincidence!" I heard myself saying, truly amazed at the amazement in my voice—then afterwards remembering we were in a library and lowering my voice almost conspiratorially. "No, I'm not related to Jeff but, believe it or not, his brother Tony up in Alaska asked me to check on him when I came down here. He hadn't heard from him in awhile and was worrying. It's really amazing that I'd meet someone who knows him as soon as I get here!"

She put both hands back on the chair and again leaned forward, obviously taken aback by the seeming coincidence, but then studying me with such a dark soberness that I was uncomfortable and thought it wasn't going to work.

"It's funny," she said, almost seeming to be talking to herself, "you sure do look like Jeff. And, he said his brother lived in Alaska, too—that he had to escape up there when he punched some newspaper reporter or something here."

"You didn't do that, did you?" she said after a pause, still more serious than light.

"No!" I said, forcing a grin. "But I do remember hearing about it."

She straightened, holding one hand to her cheek and obviously thinking some more. So that then, quickly, to break the snow balling of her logic, I took out my wallet and, pulling out the fake driver's license, extended it to her (which in retrospect I believe was another mistake).

"My name's Martin Sikorsky," I said, "and I'm flattered that you thought I was Tony Hamil. Tony's only about twenty-eight or nine, though, and doesn't have white hair like I do."

I gestured toward my head, with the license still in my hand, again succeeding to manage a plastic smile. Whereupon, and still pre-occupied, she reached and took the card, then pulled the chair out and sat on the edge of it. She studied my picture on Martin Sikorsky's supposed driver's license, periodically looking up to gaze over at me and compare. And her continued extreme seriousness in doing so was pretty disconcerting to say the least. I couldn't understand so much distrust and wondered self consciously if it were something I'd said, or if perhaps there was something about my appearance that bothered her beyond my looking like Jeff.

Still, when she finally did nod her satisfaction and hand the card back to me, I quickly seized the initiative, knowing the opportunity could be fleeting.

"Where is Jeff anyway?" I asked. "How do you happen to know him?" At which point, it was her turn to be uncomfortable.

"Well, I used to go out with him," she said rather furtively, with her eyes shifting back and forth to avoid any locked on contact—obviously less comfortable on this ground, given whatever the strain was between them.

"Used to?" I said, picking up on it, but not wanting to overstress her to the point where she might clam up. "What happened? Did old Jeff get a little weird on you? It'd be just like him!"

To which she just barely nodded, still on the edge of the chair and staring off self consciously at the stacks.

"Typical of those Vietnam vets, too," I went on. "And besides Jeff always did seem to be off in his own little world."

"You know Jeff, too?" she asked suddenly surprised and looking at me directly again, her brown eyes still registering perplexity—warning me of thought processes still going on, and the need to stay cautious.

"Yeah, well I lived at Lake Tahoe when they were kids," I said, "so I knew all of the family."

"He—he got so personal," she said softly, surprising me with the sudden intimacy—though her voice trailed off and she looked away.

"Like his feelings were the only ones that ever counted," I led her on, not without the relish of our forever sibling rivalry, but still hoping to elicit more.

She changed then, though; and, while thinking out loud, was seemingly seeing images again in her mind. Which gave me a window on what she was really all about, and brought my hostility back to the surface in a rush.

"He was such a bore," she disclosed suddenly, even angrily, "always talking about the environment and Lake Tahoe and the river and Pyramid Lake and Glenbrook—don't forget Glenbrook! And all about what the gamblers have done to this and that. I don't care! It's still better than any place I've ever been. And it seems to me the city and county governments work just fine here. My brother's a councilman, and I don't hear him complaining."

She said it proudly, defiantly—so that I could even imagine her waving a little Nevada flag—pausing for breath then, and with her dark eyes flashing. And for a moment, I was quiet as well, biting my tongue while everything in me wanted to lash out and tell her what an arrested in development imbecile I thought she really was.

She put her palms flat on the table then, as if to push herself up and presumably leave; at which point I had the presence of mind to ask her quickly about Glenbrook and her mention of it.

"What happened at Glenbrook?" I said, amazed that I somehow sounded conciliatory, and disgusted with my hypocrisy as well. "You said something about not forgetting Glenbrook."

"Oh," she said, her voice low again and controlled as she formed the words slowly, "he was going to take me to Glenbrook for dinner—to the old inn. But then, all I got to see was him throwing up."

"What?" I said, suppressing a grin and wanting to be sure I'd heard her correctly.

"Right, throwing up!" she said, resting her arms back down on the table, while leaning slightly forward, but still without eye contact, and as if she were seeing into herself. "We got to the overlook where you could see all the new condominiums. Then he got out of the car and threw up all over the place—I don't know how many times. And afterwards, just got back in the car and brought me right back down the mountain to home—without speaking or saying anything, and without even having dinner. And the ironic part of it is that, if it was the condominiums that made him so sick—and I assume it was—, he could have saved himself the trouble since they burned up just a few weeks later."

"They burned up?" I asked, not letting on I knew. "What? The condominiums?"

"Yeah, they burned up!" she said. "It should be there in that stack of papers you're looking thru."

She got up quickly then and came around the table, standing close beside me so that then I was very aware of her body and faint perfume. She leaned over to sort hurriedly thru several weeks worth of papers, then came finally to the one with the headline.

"Here it is," she said; and with a thread of fear beginning to run thru me, I leaned forward to read it, thinking for the first time that if Jeff were upset enough to throw up when he saw Glenbrook and so upset he couldn't even talk to this sensual creature standing beside me, or complete their date, then maybe anything was possible. Because first and foremost, like Ned, Jeff had *always* been polite and a gentleman around the ladies. And secondly, in Vietnam, he'd been an explosives expert—I knew—and, judging from the decorations I'd heard he received, he was very, very good.

I stared at the article unseeingly for a minute, remembering Glenbrook when we were boys, then envisioning an avenging Jeff slipping thru the forest with an army pack on his back. And I even shivered a little bit, knowing all that Indian Joe had taught us and, for the moment, forgetting about the girl—until finally, standing there, she cleared her throat.

"I'm sorry," I said, looking up, "I was just sort of remembering the old Glenbrook for a minute myself."

"And . . . ?" she asked.

"And just wondering how I'd like seeing a bunch of condos there myself."

"Well, you don't have to worry now," she said tartly. "There sure aren't any of those anymore."

"Yeah, it says here they think it was caused by a gas leak. Has there been much more about it since then?"

"No," she said, sitting then on the edge of the table, "just that they repeated it was a gas leak."

I nodded. "Well those things happen," I said, noticing in the article, too, another strong disclaimer of sabotage—which I again found intriguing.

I wanted to change the subject at that point, though, not wanting to draw any conclusions about Jeff without some serious private thinking, and especially not wanting the girl to start suspecting him as well. But then, promptly—and I can't explain such stupidity for the life of me—I turned the spotlight right back onto where I didn't want it to go.

"Say," I blurted, "when did you last see Jeff? Was it the night you went to Glenbrook for dinner?"

My words hung there in the air, but I couldn't get them back—the two questions, coming where and when they did, serving immediately to tie Jeff to the story. And, I couldn't even believe what I'd done.

And of course, she picked right up on it. "Why?" she said, putting it right out in the open. "Do you think he's involved or something?"

(And even more earnestly as she perhaps read my eyes.) "Is he in trouble?"

I shook my head. "I sure don't think so," I said. "Besides it says right here it was a gas leak."

Still, she regarded me doubtfully, even as I tried doggedly to get back on track.

"When *did* you see him last anyway?" I asked her again. "I need to find him, and his landlady hadn't seen him for awhile when I called."

"It was later on," she said, flushing then for some unaccountable reason.

"Later, after Glenbrook," I said, surprised.

"Yes," she said hesitatingly, "after he asked me to marry him. After that, and after we'd been to Virginia City."

"He proposed to you?" I almost shouted, forgetting again that we were in a library.

"Yes, he proposed to me," she said, obviously nettled by my amazed reaction and sliding down from her perch on the table to her feet.

"And, you turned him down?" I said even more incredulously.

"Yes, I turned him down," she snapped heatedly, her arms folded in front of her. "I told you he was a bore!"

"Yeah well," I said with a sigh, muttering more to myself than to her, but with my own growing anger starting to get the better of me, "maybe he didn't have any women in Vietnam."

"And, what's that supposed to mean?" she retorted, once again incensed.

"Look," I said, answering her question with questions of my own, "I don't understand why you went out with him again to Virginia City. Even after you'd decided he was a bore and you turned him down. What happened? Why *did* you go out with him again?"

Again she flushed. "Look, what is this, twenty questions?" she said, looking down again to avoid my eyes. "I don't know why. It was just different—I was different—I wanted to see . . ." Her voice trailed away again, and I couldn't fathom it, or her.

"Well, but you still found him boring?" I said.

"He . . . he got so personal," she repeated the earlier little phrase, turning bright scarlet this time. "I mean . . . he had no right."

She bowed her head, and then further surprised me by turning and hurrying suddenly out of the room.

And while I didn't know what it was about and suspected I never would, what I did know now was that Jeff had been going thru some intense emotional turmoil, what with losing *her*; the rape of Glenbrook; scars from Vietnam; the absence of our dad who'd died while Jeff was away; and no emotional support possible from either myself or Indian Joe. So that undoubtedly, he was at that point in his life a person whom I didn't even know.

I sat for a minute, sort of letting the dust settle after the girl's abrupt exit, then re-read the article about Glenbrook and the one about the boat. And I thought some about Indian Joe's letter, too, and then some more about what the girl had had to say and, more importantly perhaps, about what she hadn't said—for whatever she was holding back might have had even more of a bearing. And while Jeff's involvement in the explosions wasn't something I wanted to believe, the kernel of possibility certainly existed. So that I was experiencing the fear of it in the pit of my stomach when she came again unexpectedly and abruptly back into the room.

At once, too, she called out sharply my Alaskan name, "Bear! And not expecting it, I responded involuntarily, at least to the point of jerking my head around and very nearly answering.

"That's what they call you in Alaska, isn't it, Tony Hamil?" she said, approaching the table with a decided purposefulness, and her face with a kind of vindictive expression.

"I remember Jeff telling me that," she said. "And just to be clear, I don't believe you're Martin Sikorsky, or anyone else. I know you're Jeff's brother, and for your information, too, up close the roots of your hair aren't all white either. I could see that when I was standing next to you."

Again she gripped the chair back opposite with both hands and leaned forward, almost over me. Still in spite of the whole thing coming unraveled, I made up my mind to go ahead and pursue news of Jeff for as long as possible—pushed too, no doubt, by some deeper psychological need to have the last word.

"Where is Jeff Hamil, anyway?" I persisted, straightening up in my chair, gripping the edge of the table with both hands myself and apparently ignoring what she'd been saying. "Did you somehow have him committed to psychiatric care because he was a bore, or because he didn't think quite like everybody else? Is that what you're so uptight about?

"I'm not uptight at all!" she responded thru clenched teeth, "and I don't know where your freak of a brother is."

"Did you know Jeff was awarded for bravery in Vietnam?" I said quietly then, switching on her.

"No," she said after a pause, and bringing her own voice down. "He never talked about Vietnam. But what does that have to do with anything, anyway?"

"And did you know he blew up bridges behind enemy lines and nearly got captured by the Russians?' I went on, still quietly and still ignoring what she'd said.

"No," she said again, "but I don't see . . ."

"Not really so boring, I guess, but maybe you were so self centered, you didn't care to get it out of him. Or maybe you just would have preferred someone who'd talk to you about *his and her sprays*, and clothes on sale at the mall, instead of a man of passion and honor and commitment—who knew more about the history of the environment here than practically anyone—talking about something vital to you, the quality of your life."

"Look," she said, flustered now, and with her voice again rising dangerously, "he liked to talk, and needed to talk, I guess. And I was just there—up to a point."

"What was it?" I said, leaning forward, facing her and unleashing some of my own pent up bitterness. "Were you totally unable to cope with the idea that a man could genuinely love you? Did it seem so unnatural?"

"You talk even crazier than he did!" she snorted, her eyes full of defiance.

"Just because something is beyond you doesn't make it crazy," I returned. "I know Jeff, and that he's never given his affections away cheaply. And that he'd have never proposed to you unless he for sure loved you."

"All right, so he loved me," she snapped. "So what?"

"I just want to know what he would have had to do, really to move you?" I said, my voice again getting quiet.

At which she stiffened slightly and licked her lips, not replying for a moment, and with a look of actual confusion replacing the blazing anger. Unexpectedly too, her eyes glistened then with a welling up. But forever the product, she fought it off quickly, brushing her arm across her eyes. Then without any more discussion—without another word, in fact—turned abruptly and marched once more from the room.

Whereupon, understanding her anger, her confused sense of civic mindedness and seemingly limitless bounds of American female rationalization, I knew that a phone call to the local sheriff was about a heartbeat away. Having still the presence of mind to reach down for the briefcase, and afterwards head for the emergency exit, not interested in struggling or discussing with any other library personnel she might summons, but then setting off a deafening alarm system, as I went unsuspectingly thru the armed side door.

Outside, I was immediately, Providentially blessed to catch another city bus passing at that instant. But I had now, too, a real sickening fear starting to fill me up—fear of never seeing home or Alaska again—feeling watched and already suspected somehow by the completely oblivious other passengers. Making a quick transfer to still another bus, then within minutes arriving at the Indian reservation village South of Reno's sister city, Sparks—safe for the time being at the rundown shanty of my old school friend, Young Hunter.

Chapter Fifteen

When we were in high school, Young Hunter was a drunk, at least until we were seniors ("a drunken bum Indian," the locals would say, in amongst other comments like "those drunken bum Indians sure can't handle their fire water, ha, ha!").

The thing about Young though was that, unlike some other drunken Indians I knew, when he drank, Young got very mean and got into fights. And unlike other drunks, too, Young always won. So that finally—and I'm not sure how it came about—a local golden gloves trainer got hold of him, talked about his skills in positive, athletic terms, influenced him to quit drinking and, in due course, put him on some local cards.

Whereupon, Young Hunter won and won and won not just by decision, but always by knockout. And he became suddenly famous at school and rarest of all—accepted. An Indian who'd made it! Kids—white and Indian—went to see him fight, formed cheering sections and unfurled banners. And, Young progressed thru various tournaments and was scheduled finally to be in the Olympic Trials in San Francisco.

But then, Young didn't go—didn't show up at the train station, and no one could find him. He didn't have clothes to wear, he told me later—clothes that he thought he needed to appear in the sophisticated big city—and, also was simply and absolutely terrified of appearing country-ish, (i.e., Indian).

No one could find him for days—until the Trials were over. Then Joe found him one day drinking in a bar down on Reno's skid row. He was just turned eighteen, not twenty-one, but was Indian, so nobody could tell and nobody'd asked him for an ID in several years.

Joe, though, was not diplomatic, putting a hand on his shoulder, but speaking firmly and in English, so that no doubt some of the other patrons could hear and understand.

"You're too young to be in here," he said, "your father wants you home."

At which point Young Hunter whirled around on his stool and hit Joe with the left hook that had laid waste to all his preceding opponents. Then expecting Joe to go routinely sprawling, had to register some shock when Joe only blinked. After which, Joe taught him a swift, sure and brutal lesson in Indian combat—which Young Hunter would never forget and which, also, would wean him away and forever prejudice him against the white man's form of self defense. Then he gave up, not only boxing, but drinking once more, and came often with Joe and Jeff and myself, when we went off to camp and hunt or fish.

Young Hunter recognized me despite the passage of years and the disguise—which was not surprising, especially in that the Indians I've known always have seemed able to see past outer surface to the inner spirit.

He was thick set and dusty in gray coveralls, flat featured with tousled jet black hair—changing a tire on a battered old green pickup truck, which was pulled up in the gravel driveway alongside his typically non descript hut.

"Tony?" he said, at first a little uncertainly, then dropping his tire iron and stepping forward to shake my hand very solemnly, returning strength for strength as our eyes locked as well.

"You look like a bear now," he said. "White like you're old, though I'm not sure that's real."

"Well, Bear is what they call me now," I answered.

"Will you come inside the house, Bear?"

"Do you know I'm still wanted?"

"Well, I have no reason to think that you aren't. But, come inside."

I climbed the steps with him then, up onto a stoop, noticing how badly the little gray house was in need of paint; then passed inside as he held the door. Inside there were three rooms—a living room, kitchen and bedroom—with rough, uncarpeted plywood floors, precious little furniture and a turned on black and white TV on a stool in the corner. Also, there were five young children, I could count, in various stages of play and Young Hunter's wife, wrapped in a traditional shawl and overseeing a pot of soup on the stove.

It was noisy with chaos but, at a word from Young, the TV was snapped off and all the children along with the mother trooped off to the bedroom and closed the door. Then we sat in the kitchen on benches, facing each other across a wooden picnic table; and, opening the briefcase, I brought out Joe's letter and handed it across.

He looked at it for a moment, uncomprehendingly, then suddenly stiffened.

"Oh," he said, "Joe!"

Then unexpectedly, tears welled up in my eyes, I guess because of sharing it finally with someone who really understood. And for a few moments afterwards, neither one of us could say anything.

"I've got to get him out of there, Young," I said finally, chokingly.

"And Jeff?" he said. "What about him?"

"I don't know," I said. "Today, I tried to find out about him from a girl friend of his, and I think she may have called the police."

"Today?" he asked worriedly. "They weren't following you?"

"No, not yet," I said.

"OK, listen Tony," he said, hurriedly then and obviously rattled by this news, "there's a place you need to stay for awhile, and tonight I'll bring some of the leaders. Probably, they'll know what we can do."

He stood, motioning for me to wait, then walked out onto the porch where he stood for awhile silently, watching. By now the sun had set, though, and the few children who had been playing out front had gone in. So that afterwards, he led me out the back door and up over a dirt embankment which ran several hundred yards behind the house. Then out of sight because of the embankment, we entered a dilapidated looking old pump house in the corner of an adjoining field. In the dim light, he lit a match, then directed me to scuff the dirt away from where we were standing. Which done, revealed a trap door. The match went out, but he lit another and, as I lifted the door, he leaned over and flipped on a switch which dimly lit steps and a cement block room underneath.

There, there was a bunk bed, a table, some shelves with a little canned food, a two burner hot plate and a little refrigerator. Also, a small electric heater and an air duct up in the ceiling, as well as a small side closet with what looked like a bed pan and some bottled water.

"We have to hide some of our young people here sometimes," he explained, "when they get into trouble with drugs."

I looked back up at him, as he hadn't followed me down; and then, after he repeated that he'd be back with the others and after he lowered the trap door over me, I felt as if I'd been buried alive. I could hear him scuffing the dirt overhead to once again cover the door, and was hit then, too, with a first kernel of doubt.

'What if he wasn't what he seemed, but was in fact so fed up with white people, he'd even turn in a Hamil? And if he were to come back with the police, what chance would I have in that tomb?'

I shook off the ideas, though, not believing them; then lay down on the bed, hungry but not yet feeling able to eat their food, and too keyed up to sleep, running the events of the day back and forth thru my mind.

I thought of the girl, angrily. It was typical to have a know nothing like her wind up sitting in judgment, I knew, stepping forward willingly to put the fate of someone else —in this case mine—in dire jeopardy. And while I could wish that she hadn't done so, in my heart I knew that she had—having nothing in her head to draw from other than a cliché ridden loyalty to society's agenda, in this case manufactured and instilled by the most cynical of community leaders, the Nevada mob.

By turning me in, though, and rejecting Jeff the radical, she actually was choosing a safe ignorance, able to feel good about herself for doing the "correct" thing—when in reality the system she was *aiding and abetting* was the very fountain of corruption and, in this case, the fountain of her corrupted thinking.

I thought Jeff had known that—must have realized it about her—and yet had let himself get involved anyway. And while her defiant remarks about not caring what the gamblers did indicated he'd probably done everything he could to turn her around, unfortunately I was sure he'd failed.

I did doze off for a little while then, afterwards waking up and for a moment not knowing where I could be. Then, I heard renewed scuffing sounds overhead and, coming more fully awake, wondered again briefly about the police.

Immediately though, there came instead a procession down the narrow steps of several older Indians and, of course, Young Hunter. Dark skinned, mostly heavy set and, in some cases, still sweating from the day's work, they milled around momentarily while I sat on the edge of the bunk looking up at them. And then, one by one they shook my hand, before squatting on the floor around me—seeming in the dim light like some convened ghost council from the past, but with members disguised now in baggy hand-me-down white man's trousers and faded denim shirts. Some, I knew from long before, and because of Indian Joe and my grandparents who'd raised Indian Joe. And because of my dad, Ned, I knew they all knew me.

"You didn't eat," one of them, the smallest and skinniest, with a white man's name, Ray Jamison, noticed.

"Not yet," I said.

"You can, you know," he said. "We all know you, and you will always be welcomed here."

I nodded, feeling a warmth of appreciation. "I'm just sorry to bring trouble," I said.

"You didn't bring trouble," he returned, immediately serious. "Joe sent for you."

Then, for a few moments there was silence. Followed by a much deeper voice coming from a white haired old man off to my left. I knew him nominally as their leader—the tribal chairman—though I couldn't recall his Indian name.

"What do you want to do?" he said in his deep bass. "What do you propose?"

"I want to find out if my brother's alive," I said, "and I want to get Joe out."

And again there was silence for what seemed a good minute.

"Getting Joe out from there will not be easy," the old man said finally. "We have never been able to figure a way, and we know your father tried all legal means."

"Legal!" I spat the word back at him, perhaps surprising them with my anger. "There is no legal here."

"No," the old man said, slowly, "but there is power, and we have to live under it—we, and our children, if we are to live at all."

And again there was silence, as each considered that thought.

"And what about your brother?" a younger, but extremely heavy man to my right finally asked. "How can you find out if what Joe said is true?"

And I told them—told them of having the phone number of the rooming house where Jeff had been staying—of trying to call him there right after receiving Joe's letter, and before leaving Alaska. Related the landlady's response that she hadn't seen Jeff in over a month and that he hadn't paid his rent either—and then of calling her once more from my aunt's house that day and receiving the same answer again.

"Maybe you should go by there and look thru his things," Young Hunter spoke from his seat across from me on the steps. "Maybe you could get some idea from that."

"Well, I was going to do that," I said, "until—like I told you—his girl friend recognized me today."

"And you're sure she turned you in?" the old man asked in his deep tones.

"She was the type,"

"And how did Jeff select her?"

"I was just lying here, wondering that very thing. I guess he was lonesome."

"Jeff knew better, though," the old man said with a tinge of disgust. "And it's not your fault—you couldn't have expected her to be like that."

I nodded, grateful, but then not agreeable to his next suggestion.

"I think you must stay here for many days," the old man said, "until they've forgotten you. Then maybe you can see about your brother—and about Joe."

Still, I didn't dissent immediately in deference to his stature and wisdom.

Another Indian spoke first, essentially agreeing with the old man, though suggesting also that the mountains of the Pyramid Lake Reservation might be a better place for me to hide if they could get me there. 'There, there were many caves,' he said, 'and I'd be free to move about and also to hunt for game until such time as it was deemed safe.'

They spoke in the Indian language then, planning—the main consideration being how to get me out of Reno—and with my remembering enough of their tongue to get just the gist of it. They could hide me in the back of a truck in some hay, they thought, or we could go by horseback, or if necessary by foot at night. And remembering that the reservation was about thirty miles away thru the desert, I knew that in several respects it made more sense for me to be there. Especially from their point of view, it would be safer for all concerned; still it wasn't at all what I had in mind.

I took out my wallet then, as I'd done for the girl in the library, but instead of the fake license I showed them a picture of the Aleut and our son, passing it first to the heavy Indian on my left.

"This is my wife and my son," I said, "and I don't want to be long away."

The Indian leaned back so that the light from the dim bulb fell on the picture; then having studied it, passed it on with a nod of approval to the old man who was on his left. And, this went on until all had seen it.

"Is she Aleut? Your wife?" the old man asked.

"Yes," I said.

"I have heard these people have a weakness for drink," the old man said, "the same as we do."

"Yes, that's true," I said. "Especially the men."

"But not your wife."

"No."

"That's good then," the old man said, nodding his approval.

I nodded, too, and then they were all silent again, waiting I knew for me to say more.

"I know it's dangerous now," I said, "and I know it's the smart way—the Indian way—to hole up and to strike later when it's not expected. But I know, too, this may be the opportune time. It may be the only time. If they've got Jeff, or if they've killed him, now's when they're going to be covering things up—when they think someone may be coming. And if I wait until later, everything *will* be covered up, and it will be that much harder to find things out. Besides that, if they have Jeff now but haven't killed him yet, but are planning to, the longer I wait, the greater the chance he'll be dead when I get there."

They listened in silence and, I knew, with respect for my logic. I could feel it and appreciated it. And I went on.

"What I want to do, is get to Lake Tahoe. I want to see Glenbrook and figure out if Jeff caused that explosion there, and where he went afterwards. And if he blew up the boat at Zephyr Cove, and where he went after that. Who knows? If he did those things, he could still be hiding in the mountains—or maybe he's lying up wounded somewhere."

I looked around at their dark faces, all studying me intently. Then I spoke again.

"The other thing, I want to do, is sneak Joe out of that hospital and take him back with me—to Alaska. I know that's not going to be easy, but I do have quite a lot of money we can use. And if you know anyone who works at that hospital, or anyone who knows anyone who works there, when I come back from Lake Tahoe, we can try to get next to them."

At which point, the leader turned and said something else in their language, then seemingly was challenged by another of the group—a younger, heavy set man to my right, who was particularly forceful and demonstrative, gesturing with both hands, and with his comments drawing murmurs of approval from some of the others.

"Tony," the chief said, at length returning his attention to me, "you see, times are changing here. Now there is talk of the gambling men forming a partnership with our people. Of putting one of their casinos on our lands, and sharing the profits. The older Indians are resisting this idea, but the younger ones are demanding change and believe it is the only way to escape our poverty. They (and he nodded his head towards the younger man who had spoken so forcefully) want to help you rescue Joe, but are much concerned with risking the new possibilities. And I, as their leader, am torn as well, knowing the deceit of the gambling men, but with much difficulty defending the poverty of our lives."

"Tony" he said after a pause, " your family has been our family more than all other people here, and for that reason it grieves us deeply that you won't do the prudent thing and stay for a time in the rocks at Lake Pyramid, or even here, until it is safe. But we understand, too, about the uncertainty for your brother and about your concerns for your wife and your young son; and we know that as a man you must do certain things. Tomorrow, we will make a plan for getting you to Lake Tahoe."

And with that said, he stood up, as did the others, each shaking my hand again before filing back up the cement steps.

Young Hunter, being the youngest, though, stepped aside waiting to go last, and I used the opportunity to ask him about a gun.

"Young," I said quietly, "I'd intended to buy a gun, but right now you know I can't go in the stores. Can you get me one?"

"What do you want, Tony?" he asked.

"A thirty-thirty brush gun without a scope."

He stood, facing me, I remember, with his black eyes regarding me soberly.

"Well, I have one of those you can have, Tony," he said, "but I'm surprised you don't want a scope."

"If I'm going to have to shoot someone, Young," I said, "I'll want them to be close enough to know who I am."

And afterwards—after he'd followed after the others and then been gone for awhile—he came back with the rifle and a full cartridge belt, steadfastly refusing to take any money from me.

Chapter Sixteen

Together, Young Hunter and I tracked a mountain lion once, when we were in high school and friends. When we finally cornered it in a steep walled box canyon, neither of us could shoot. It was the only one we'd ever seen and was too wonderful to kill.

As the moment passed and neither of us fired, the cat—which was only about fifty yards away—regarded us curiously. He opened his mouth, emitting a deep growl, then startled us by trotting then accelerating directly towards the thin stand of trees where we were hiding. I tried to draw down on him then, as did Young Hunter; but, just that suddenly, he swerved off into the brush and was gone.

In the early light of morning, we wound our way up the torturous climbing Mt. Rose highway, smelling the pine trees before seeing them, and passing the cleared, but boulder-strewn slopes beneath the seasonally idled ski lifts. Reaching the summit about the time the sun was breasting the Eastern range—to be greeted by the dazzling view of *Da ow ga*, the great blue Lake, opening out beneath us. Then beside me, Young Hunter steered the battered old green truck with great care into the descent, braking often down the steep slope as we twisted thru large hairpin turns, punctuated by panoramic scenes of lake, mountains and trees.

Now I was dressed and disguised as a Paiute Indian, complete with herbal dyed face, neck, arms and hands, my beard gone and my white hair rinsed Indian jet black. This, because Young Hunter had caught me around midnight in the darkness, trying to slip away from the pump house, unaccompanied; and had been able after no small struggle to convince me to do otherwise.

I'd lain on the bunk in the underground concrete room and, the more I'd thought about things, the more uneasy I'd become. What I was doing was putting the whole Indian tribe at risk—something they definitely didn't need—and feeling more secure then because of Young's rifle, I'd finally made up my mind to do things on my own.

Right at midnight, I'd lifted up the trap door and, with gun in one hand, briefcase in the other and cartridge belt slung across my shoulder, had moved stealthily out into the darkness towards the earthen embankment. Then, heard a voice—a muffled sound which seemed to float up out of the darkness with no body attached, but which froze me, all the same.

"Stand real still," were the words, "and lay the rifle down on the ground."

And not knowing who it was, and unable even to consider shooting at someone I couldn't see, I did as I was told.

Then, Young Hunter spoke in his recognizable voice.

"Gotcha Tony!" he said. "Sneakin' out on us, eh?"

At which point I loudly expelled my held breath, relieved and understanding that they'd known I'd try not to implicate them further, and so had posted a guard, having determined now to help me regardless of what I decided.

"Darn Young," I muttered, "you sure would have had me."

To which he replied coolly, his voice still disconnected from any discernible body. "Don't try to get friendly now, Bear. We're onto the old hit the Indian over the head and run trick, too. So, you can either go back to bed, or you and I can get started for Lake Tahoe together."

"Well," I said slowly. "I don't know. Could you leave with me now?"

"Yeah," he said, "we threw dice last night after we left you, and I won the honor of driving you. And that's how we look on it, Tony, as an honor."

"Well, but that's the thing," I said, "if I were just to cut cross country on foot and travel at night, there'd be no worry about anyone seeing me. And, I wouldn't be involving any of you either."

"We're already involved, Tony," he responded, "because of Joe. And it's more than fifty miles to Lake Tahoe on foot. More than fifty miles over some very tall mountains."

"I know how far it is," I argued testily, "but it wouldn't take me more than two or three nights, and there'd be no risk at all."

"Yeah, if your feet didn't swell up and blister and all the skin peel off. Then, what good would you be?"

At which point, for a moment, we were both silent—I with my looming hulk still standing motionless by the pump house, and with the rifle on the ground; and Young Hunter out somewhere else in the darkness.

"Besides," he said at length, "who was it that made the point at the meeting tonight that time's short?"

"Well, maybe I've had a change of heart since then," I returned weakly.

"Yeah well, I guess we could always re-convene the Council," he said with a suppressed chuckle, "and tell them you decided you had time after all—enough time to walk to Lake Tahoe. And then, they'd all say 'that was good and that, if you had that much time, it wouldn't hurt a bit for you to hide out for awhile at Lake Pyramid either'."

"Tony," he said, appearing then suddenly and surprisingly right beside me without any weapon and putting a friendly hand on my shoulder, "the bad news is you're a TV star now. They've done a composite drawing of you and put it on all the channels, saying you're wanted for questioning on some very serious charges, and that you're to be considered armed and dangerous. And also, they give your name and the name you're assumed to be traveling under, Martin Sikorsky. So, I think you might need our help after all."

And, as the weight of his words hit me, I had a sinking feeling in the pit of my stomach, though at that point I didn't analyze it fully—didn't question the full significance of an all channel bulletin about someone who'd merely had a fist fight six years earlier. Rather, all I did at first was just to mutter that the girl really had done a number on me, and that the danger she'd created was additional reason why no one ought to come with me. Then, I picked up the rifle and started climbing up the embankment; and, although Young climbed, too, right beside me, for a moment it was as if he'd ceased to exist. Because truth to tell, my legs were feeling rubbery and weak, and an icy fear very like panic was gripping my insides.

Thinking about it, too, in retrospect, I have to believe it had partly to do with where I'd come from. Because, as a fish boat captain in Alaska, I'd developed in my mind a certain invincibility and, also, a contempt for those living the soft, contemporary life style of 'the lower forty-eight.' So that when I'd decided to respond to Joe's letter and go there, I think it just hadn't occurred to me—at least not on a deep down gut level—that I could lose. Joe's letter had said "come" and so, of course, I was going there to liberate him. Period and simple as that.

But now, circumstances were changing things—chipping away at that confidence and filling me with more doubt than I'd ever expected. And on the dark side, too, and more immediately, I thought it would be only a matter of time before someone remembered about the Hamil's ties to the Indians and would come rooting around, looking for me there in the village. Then anything might happen, I knew; and, from the pump house bunker, there were no mountains to run to.

"OK, Young," I said, deciding suddenly after we'd reached the top of the bunker, "Let's do it now!"

Whereupon, standing facing me atop the bank, still obscure in the darkness but with arms folded across his chest, he brought forth still another consideration.

"Tony," he said, "I understand your impatience, but this may save your life. The chief and all of us think that you should shave off your beard. I know that your skin will be real white under there, but my wife's got some herbal dye that'll make you the color of one of us, and we can re-dye your hair black like ours as well."

Which once again caused me to hesitate, as feeling the adrenaline surging thru me and wanting then to be away, I nevertheless remembered some long ago words from Joe about always having the advantage before going into battle. Which caused me to acquiesce again, as bowing my head in submission, I followed him back inside his kitchen.

He brought scissors and a straight edge and, in short order, I had the beard off, my skin underneath hot feeling and bleeding from several nicks and scratches. After which, he went away in his truck to an all night grocery, leaving me in the house with his sleeping family and bringing back a black dye rinse for my hair which I applied in the *no choice*, cold water shower. Then, Young's wife, Quiet Dawn, got up and brought the brown Indian dye, helping me to apply it, not only to my face, neck, arms and hands, but also pointing insistently to my chest and belly.

And while I at first resisted when she tugged at the front of my shirt—her rough hands somehow gentle and caring, contrasted to her flat features which were typically stolid and without emotion—it was Young who again put things into perspective.

"Young," I said, "don't you think my face and hands are enough?"

"Sometimes," he said—and his response was slow and very grave—"the God speaks to her. And I have found it always best to do as she says."

And yielding once more, I took off my shirt and, after she modestly proffered the jar of dye, again rubbed it in vigorously. While Young Hunter went off someplace yet another time, later to re-appear with a large, battered gray stetson, old cowboy boots, tattered jeans and an extra large, long-sleeve blue shirt. Whereupon, with my changing into them, my transformation was complete.

"Just another bum Indian on his way in the morning to his minimum wage day," Young Hunter said bitingly, similarly attired in gray Stetson, jeans and work shirt. Instructing his wife, also, and prior to any search and questioning, to burn my discarded things—all but the briefcase with the money, which we buried out behind the pump house, and the brush boots which I'd come with, and which I took along for our expected hike.

At Lake Tahoe—at the bottom of the grade, at Incline Beach—we turned South towards Glenbrook, which was still a good twenty miles distant; and, all the while, I kept thinking about the bulletin on television, and about courage, and about what I'd come to do. I thought about Jeff, wondering if in fact he might be alive. And then Young—thinking along similar lines—asked why I thought they'd had me on TV.

"Do you think they've already connected you to the bombings, Tony?" he said. "And wouldn't that mean they know Jeff did it, and maybe have him already?"

And thinking again about the passage of years since the fight, and the relatively inconsequential conversation with the girl, I had to agree.

"Maybe, they *have* killed Jeff," I said, "and don't want me to find out."

"Yeah, unless maybe the girl just told them you thought Jeff did the bombing. You did say the idea struck you both about the same time."

"Well, that's a possibility," I said more doubtfully, "And for Jeff's sake, let's hope it's true. At least in that case he still could be alive."

We traveled on, mostly in silence again, driving slowly with our thoughts, and with the windows down, smelling the forest. Then finally when I spoke again, the focus was shifted.

"Young," I said, "if you'd just blown up Glenbrook, where would you go to hide?"

He looked at me, his dark round face suddenly blank. "You mean if I had a car, or a boat, or what?" he said.

"Well, let's put it another way," I returned. "If you were the authorities and somebody just blew up Glenbrook, what would you do first?"

"Well, I'd seal all the roads out of the basin and put cutters out patrolling the Lake—stopping boats and checking docks. And I'd close the airport and hope whoever it was didn't have a sea plane."

"Exactly," I said, "but what if the guy was on foot?"

And, again he looked blank.

"Well, I don't think he would be. He'd be looking to get out fast."

"But what if he figured the police would think that way and stayed on foot? Pull over for a minute, Young."

I took out the area map I'd seen him put in the glove box as we were leaving and, opening it, pointed out Glenbrook. "When we were kids, you know we lived there every summer, Young," I said, "and lots of times Joe would come there and hike with us. We'd hike up here (I said, pointing), up along an old rail bed they used to use for hauling logs up to the summit. There was a big flume up there in the old days, and they could shoot the logs from there all the way down to Carson City.

"But sometimes, we'd go on longer hikes and stay overnight up here at Marlette Lake. And once, I remember going on an even longer hike back up to what's called Hobart Reservoir.

' "Right here," I said, pointing to an all but invisible blue dot. "Joe showed us an old Indian cave there, I remember, with some buried rabbit hides; and I'll bet anything, after Glenbrook, that's where Jeff went to hide out."

We sat then, regarding the map in silence for awhile, and it was becoming easier for me to visualize it—easier to put myself in Jeff's body.

"But, what about the boat and Zephyr Cove?" Young wanted to know after awhile, finally putting the truck in gear and pulling back onto the highway. "Hobart Dam's a long way from there. He wouldn't have gone all the way back there again, if he blew up the boat, too."

"Well, that's what I'm getting at," I returned.

"You're right! After Zephyr Cove, he probably would have gone straight into the mountains there instead of back to the North—so, if we're going to find any trace of him now, it'll be in those mountains, and not up out of Glenbrook.

Directly then, we were passing the junction with Spooner's Summit Highway, which came up out of Carson City; and soon after that were approaching the Glenbrook overlook—giving rise to all sorts of butterflies of expectation. On the edge of a flood of memories, expecting it to be as it had always been, but at the same time dreading to see the difference.

"Do you want to stop?" Young Hunter asked; and for a moment I hesitated, asking finally that he just slow down in case of it's being watched.

Then I exhaled with a sick feeling, as we rolled slowly along the turnout's edge.

"It's burned black, Young!" I related, "All of it! All except the old inn and the two big gold poplars out in front by the Lake!"

I stared at the horror of it, the desolate scene forever etched in my brain; and afterwards, as we immediately drove on, I was struck with the irony of it—'that Jeff should do such a thing to the place he'd loved best.'

"How the world turns, Young!" I sighed finally; and in the horror of the observation, there was then, too, a more heightened awareness of the reality, and of the dangers attendant to it.

Chapter Seventeen

After another several miles of pine forest, we came to Zephyr Cove Resort, choosing not to turn down to the pier where the boat, *Tahoe Dixie,* had been moored, but rather pulling off into the pines and quaking aspen across from the old log cabin lodge and restaurant.

It being mid autumn, there were few people around and after changing footgear—Young from cowboy boots to running shoes, and I into my low cut walking boots—Young unlocked the big tool box up behind the cab. He glanced around to see that we were alone, then pulled our weapons from under his various tools, handing me down the 30/30 and cartridge belt, then sticking his old, long barreled .45 revolver in his belt. He also shouldered our pack which had a small camp shovel lashed to the outside and which contained various necessities, including his jacket, the lunches his wife had made, some instant coffee in a plastic bag, bacon, small skillet, light weight aluminum pot, matches, flashlight, tin plates and cups. While I had only the rifle slung over one shoulder and the cartridge belt and a second jacket over the other.

As we started East towards the mountains, too, we could see the riding stables off to the left and even debated taking horses, especially in view of my not being used to the high altitude; but then decided against it, as a sign announced "day trips only". In the event we had to stay out longer than a day, there'd be unwanted attention, and so we had to decline.

Very soon too in our hiking, we encountered the myriad of crossing and re-crossing switchback horse trails; and immediately Young Hunter was understanding.

"That boat explosion was at night, wasn't it?" he asked.

"Yeah," I grunted, already breathing hard, "that's what the article in the paper said."

"So, how would you have *liked* to have set those charges and been trying to get away fast and run into all these looping trails in the dark? Or did you guys play over here, too, when you were kids."

"No, you know," I said, "we never did. And I bet Jeff did have some time with all this circling around. Probably, after awhile he just set his compass by the stars and headed straight on up, breaking thru manzanita and climbing over rocks until it got light enough for him to see."

"Yeah, and I bet he came face to face with some of these big sugar pines before the night was out, especially if it was real dark and there was no moon."

We slogged on then, ever upward, pausing often though because of my shortness of breath—climbing down on rocks on occasion to drink from the cascading white water stream which rushed endlessly back down the slope towards the Lake. And the hours passed, as did the miles—slowly. And we saw nothing, or at least not anything we could be sure of, as what signs we did run across—for example, a gum wrapper and a book of matches—could have been left by anyone. Given the time lapse, there was no way of knowing. And at one point, I made the remark that all we really could look for was Jeff's body—either dead or alive.

Noon came and we paused in among some large black boulders for lunch. A single tall pine shaded us slightly and, after we'd eaten the egg sandwiches that Young's wife had fixed, we sat in a sort of silent torpor, with the sun glaring brightly, crickets buzzing somewhere, and with the wind high up in the lone tree creating a faraway background murmuring like surf on a shore.

'It was so deceptive,' I thought, just as I was dozing—'this peacefulness with danger underneath.' And, I wondered if, when Jeff had passed there, he might have been thinking the same thing.

Soon, Young had us up again, though, swinging back onto the trail, which by this time had straightened out into one entity—ascending around boulders and cutting thru shiny green manzanita—with tree stands thinning as we reached higher and higher elevations. Nor was it all climbing, as each steep ascent seemed to be followed by a steep descent, which sometimes made me wonder why we'd climbed up in the first place.

My heart pounded with the strain of trying to keep up, as the high altitude was taking its toll. My borrowed work clothes were long since soaked full with sweat, as the strain of dragging my big body over those mountains made the desire to stop and rest a constant. Several times I felt my legs cramping and, if Young Hunter hadn't dropped back and got salt out of the pack for me to put on my tongue—an old Indian remedy that unfailingly caused cramps to subside—I might have given up entirely.

We hiked on endlessly—thru the long afternoon—until after six o'clock when the sun had just set and we came up on a high meadow. Where halfway across, Young Hunter stopped suddenly and motioned for me to come forward.

When I got up with him, he was bending over a torn scrap of clothing—what looked to be a piece of army fatigue green khaki. It was just a small scrap really, and would have seemed insignificant and perhaps gone unnoticed except in the context in which we were searching. But then in another twenty paces or so, we found an additional piece, and this one was bigger and stained apparently with blood. Then, there was the onset of a growing horror, and I felt I didn't want to go on at all—wanted to turn away and go back to where we'd come from. And squatting and holding the bloodied remnant in his hand, Young Hunter looked up at me with the same grim despair in his eyes, his dark Indian visage etched then forever in my memory and against the forever backdrop of the rose tinged sky and field.

We moved forward, though, without a word, like automatons—then found my brother's body, or what was left of it, over in among a patch of boulders.

Animals had gotten at the body, tearing away pieces of flesh and, in the process, the clothing as well. The entrails were mostly eaten, though six or eight vultures were feasting as we walked up—flying off grudgingly, but landing again not far away and waiting expectantly. And, the stench was so unbearable that Young Hunter threw up involuntarily and moved off slightly upwind, though I felt myself unable to do the same. In spite of the sight and smell, I needed to get even closer—to touch Jeff and comfort him somehow.

I held the borrowed jacket against my nose and dropped down to my knees beside him, reaching out a hand to touch his shoulder which was still covered by what was left of the shirt. My eyes were watering badly, though, and it was hard to see. Still, it wasn't difficult to make out the hole thru the center of his forehead caused by a bullet's entry, and I knew the exit hole behind must be much larger still. Also, there was white mucus-like brain matter oozing from the edges; his eyes had been pecked out by birds; and his hands and feet remained tightly bound with nylon cord.

Without even knowing what I was doing, I got up then and moved away to the edge of the meadow, my mind blurred and in some kind of automatic state. I sat down on a log underneath some pine trees and held my head in my hands for a long while, and I didn't try to think, or to direct my mind to think, needing, I guess, a settling out period, or time for assimilating the altered circumstances. I sat picking up clods of dirt and squeezing them into powder over and over again—until darkness finally came and settled over the meadow.

A sliver of moon appeared to the West, and then finally I was roused by the new horror of snarls and tearing animal sounds, which at least re-instilled some purpose in me—the purpose to bury him right then and regardless of consequences, regardless of strategy and considerations of personal safety; ahead of remembering when we were boys together; and finally ahead of just everything.

I got up and called in a low, croaking voice to Young Hunter, vaguely surprised when he responded from a sitting position on the ground right alongside.

"I've got to bury him, Young," I said, "and I don't care who finds out."

And he answered softly that he understood.

"I'll hold the light," he said, rustling around for it in the pack. Then afterwards, we moved together back out into the meadow and towards the terrible growling noises.

Paired yellow eyes, possibly of a bobcat, glowed balefully at us from the darkness near the body, but forms indistinct blurred in flight as the beamed light sought identity. Then I dug furiously in the ground with the little shovel, driven and pressured by the horror of death and the overpowering stench, but also by the place's hostility, and the animals themselves.

I dug deeply in the sandy soil despite the smallness of the blade, then finally was confronted with the problem of getting the rotting corpse intact down into the hole. What I needed was a piece of plyboard to slip underneath, but of course there wasn't any plyboard there. Young Hunter suggested the alternative of pine boughs, though; and, while I took a turn holding the light, proceeded to gather up several which we managed to work at intervals in under Jeff's body. Then, with the light hung up in some brush, we pulled the bough ends so that boughs and body slid slowly down into the grave. I spaded the earth back in on top and afterwards, as defense against the animals, we carried and rolled boulders over to cover the site. And I notched two twigs with Young's knife to make a cross and placed it at the head.

Then still in silence and a few dozen yards away, we made camp in a stand of pines. Young Hunter got some water from a seep and boiled it for coffee, which we drank against the chilling mountain air, and before lying down on pine bough beds near the fire, each with thoughts of our own.

I looked up at the stars bright in the high mountain air, still in shock, I suppose, and drowning in the horror of it—trying to focus on individual stars and remember their Indian names as Jeff and I had done when we were young and camping in similar places. Vaguely, I remembered how Joe had taught us Indian legends regarding certain stars, but with my mind skittish and not able to stay with such thought. When we were young in like places, we would listen to the wind and the night sounds and think of the fishing or hunting we'd done, or were going to do. And remembering, I couldn't sleep, and couldn't stand to lie there awake either; so that then, I got back up and stood with my back to the diminishing fire, head down and grieving in the darkness, again barely aware of the flickering shadows and light. I don't know how long I stood that way either, unaware even of the stiffness growing in my trail weary joints—awash and merely existing then in a dark sea of regrets.

Later, when the otherworldly howlings of a pack of coyotes got thru to me, I wasn't sure how long they'd been going on, and noticed only that they were very close by, probably in the vicinity of the grave. I moved to throw more wood on the glowing remnant of the fire, which produced a shower of sparks, then a single yelp from the pack, and afterwards a receding of their yips and barkings. After which, I tried lying down again but, with the horror and grief remaining, could only wait on the pine boughs for dawn.

Gradually too, as some of the shock began to subside, there was a terrible kindling of my old hate and anger—which may seem strange to say, as one might expect that to be automatically a part of the mix. But I think people are affected differently by trauma, and my first response had been simply sorrow for Jeff and emptiness. The more I thought of Jeff, though, and about what a really good guy he was, and how our whole family had stood for what was right and decent, and how good the country had been— all despoiled by the relentless greed of the gangster politicians—, there was a rising up in me, as I say, which soon became a choking, blood lust need to kill.

I didn't know how I'd bring about such vengeance, but I had the strong intuition that Jeff's killers were going to come back, primarily because they'd left Jeff unburied, and because I was known to be in the area now—for unstated reasons and with no one exactly sure what, if any, kind of power I might be bringing with me. So that logically, covering their tracks now would become a priority.

I thought when it got light Young Hunter and I could build blinds in which to wait in ambush, knowing that Young would want us to do that, as would the tribe. And while after a time, there started in me, too, a little voice of reason, reminding that in spite of my hostility I'd never been a killer—hadn't come there to kill but only to help Joe *and* Jeff (*if he were alive*), and that my real life was in Alaska with the Aleut and our baby son—still I made the conscious effort to ignore all such ideas, at least for the time.

Chapter Eighteen

Once Jeff sent me a letter from Viet Nam. He'd just come out from behind enemy lines—from the Ho Chi Minh Trail—where he and another demolition expert, named Miller, had been blowing up enemy bridges. If it weren't for Miller, he said, he wouldn't have made it out alive.

Miller was a little man, scrawny and inconspicuous; but, in combat, a remorseless killer with ice water for blood. They called him, "Ice", in fact—a man who, Jeff said, would never be able to function in normal society, but who, within the context of war, was the very best.

In the early light cold, Young Hunter and I ate bacon, which Young had fried, and drank more coffee. Then we spoke finally for the first time.

"Do you think they'll come back, Tony?" the Indian asked. "Today?"

And I said that I did. "I'm surprised they weren't here already," I said, "ahead of us. Because the hired guns who did the job on Jeff and then were too lazy to bury him, but probably told their bosses they did, are going to be real anxious to get back up here and make it clean."

"And what's going to happen when they find the job's already been done for them?" the Indian said.

"I don't know," I said uneasily. "I'm not sure."

Shivering against the early cool, we squatted near the fire, coffee mugs warming our hands, both thinking, considering.

"Will you kill them, Tony?" Young said after awhile, a question which I didn't immediately answer.

"They came with a helicopter, you know?" he said. "Did you notice that?"

"No," I said, suddenly interested. "How do you know that?"

He motioned for me to come with him—out of the stand of trees into the meadow and not far from the rocks we'd piled over Jeff's grave. There the grass had been flattened down by the action of a rotor, and tire marks were plainly visible in the sand.

"So?" the Indian asked.

"So," I said, "that's how they caught up to him. And even then he must have heard them coming."

"Yeah, I wonder if Jeff didn't just want to die."

Again we were silent, walking in a slow circle, searching for other signs, but not finding any.

"So what, Young?" I said at length. "What do you think?"

"I think they could be on us very quickly with their helicopter," he said. So that then, we went back and snuffed out the fire.

It was at that point, too, that the voice of reason began to get the upper hand, and I suggested that we might ought to leave.

"Young, killing these guys, or whoever did it, isn't going to bring Jeff back," I said. "And we could get killed ourselves trying"—regretting immediately my phrasing, as I knew it could be construed as cowardice.

At first too, he just looked at me, without expression and waiting for me to say more.

"I'd rather stay alive and at least help Joe get out," I explained, "instead of risking everything for you and me both on a situation that's already lost."

Still he didn't say anything, but followed my lead in picking up our camp, washing up the two pots and few utensils at the seep and replacing them in the pack.

We didn't leave, though, and probably in retrospect that would have been the time to have done so. But there was this thing between us—this unresolved conflict—and I wasn't even sure that, if I'd left, Young would have gone with me.

Partly because of my own indecision, and partly for something to do, I began constructing a blind on the edge of the tree stand nearest Jeff's grave, using the shovel to scrape out a depression in the clay under some manzanita and dragging over some dead pine boughs to lay across the top. And pretty soon, in silence, Young Hunter did the same thing nearby, handing me the 30/30 to put inside my hole and taking care of the pack in his.

We lay up quiet afterwards and basically rested from the rigors of the preceding day, surveying the meadow, but with a kind of lethargy and still without speaking. And I resolved that if no one showed up by six o'clock that evening, I'd go back, regardless of what Young thought or did.

The day dragged by endlessly and there was nothing—only the stillness of the high meadow; the occasional sound of a cricket, empty and lonesome as in a vacuum; and the distant rising and falling of the wind high above us in the pines. Then at noon, even the crickets and the wind ceased, and there was only the glare from the sun.

I got out, walked around awhile, and carved on some twigs with my knife; while Young Hunter sat outside with legs crossed, though still surveying the meadow—until finally at two o'clock in the afternoon when, I think, Young had all but given up hope, and my hope was intensifying that nothing would happen, we heard suddenly the distinctive clatter of a chopper and dove back into the blinds.

In a matter of moments, too, looking up thru the narrow gaps in the boughs, I could see the black and white copter, as it hovered before pitching down. And I felt my heart pumping as I never had before in my life—never on deck in a storm in the Bering Sea, or in a bar room brawl with the Russians, or before squeezing the trigger on my first buck deer. Never! Never had I felt such a dark fear, and there was scant comfort in my tight grip on the wooden stock of the 30/30.

The helicopter rocked to a stop; the rotor blade slowed, then stopped; and very shortly two men got down, one short and swarthy in a black jump suit, and the other—the pilot, I thought— taller and red haired with white coveralls. Both were carrying rifles, which looked to be M-16's, though at that distance I couldn't be exactly sure; and both men assumed crouching, military postures immediately, pivoting and sweeping thru a full three-sixty scan with an aggressive professionalism which made my blood run cold.

"Well, I don't see anybody," the blacksuit said, as they both relaxed momentarily after not having drawn fire.

"Though that doesn't mean they aren't around," he went on, his voice carrying easily over the forty or so yards to where we were hiding.

The two of them examined Jeff's grave then, and the ground around it, walking in a circle before the one in white spoke up.

"I don't know," he said. "It's kind of spooky ain't it? I mean, who'd have thought way out here the dude would already be put in the ground?"

Blacksuit grunted.

"Do you think we ought to dig him up?" he was asked.

"What for?" he said, absently pulling my twig cross out of the ground and flinging it away. "Just so we can bury him again. We already know he's dead, and now we know it's all cleaned up. So, why sweat it?"

"Well, I don't know. It seems like maybe we ought to move him. Then if it comes up in court or something, whoever buried him won't be able to come back here and produce the body."

And Blacksuit was quiet, considering. "Well," he said finally, "you may have a point there. But on the other hand, that body's going to be rotting now. The flesh'll be pulling off the bones and the stench'll kill ya! I don't want to move it, I can tell you that, and I sure don't want to put it in the bird." He paused, then went on. "Besides, as far as anyone back there is concerned, we've done our job. We killed him, right? And buried him. And if someone else found him, it's not our fault. Besides, anyone goes to court with a case like this is just going to lose."

He winked broadly, then afterwards they walked around the grave some more without speaking.

"It is funny, though" Blacksuit spoke again at length, I wonder who did bury him? Just some hiker, you think? Who could've known he was here? Remember what he said—what he kept sayin'—'that the clubs had him do it'—I wonder who did put him up to it?"

"I don't know," Whitesuit said, "but this grave looks pretty fresh dug to me. Whoever did it may still be around."

"Yeah, let's go back up in the air and scout around a few miles. If we see anybody hikin', we can drop down and check'em out."

And from the brush, I thought about shooting them—considered it throughout their conversation which proved them to be Jeff's killers—considered it with one burning, angry, hating part of me wanting a swift, sure avenging of my brother's death. But with that small voice of reason still with me, reminding that it really wouldn't be that at all, in that it wouldn't touch those who had ordered Jeff's killing, or brought him to the state he'd been in.

I knew that Young Hunter lying flat in the other bunker thought differently and probably was expecting me to shoot, wanting to join in himself. But again, I was stopped because I knew it wasn't who I was; and, if I killed cold bloodedly, realized it would change me forever and change what I had with the Aleut and our young son, too, even assuming I got back to them.

Still, as I say, at more than one point as I listened to them, I leaned the other way and, twice as I tightened my finger on the trigger, Scripture, which my mother had taught me, flashed in my mind.

"Vengeance is mine, saith the Lord," was one, and the other: *"Today, I put before you a blessing and a curse; choose life."*

Ultimately, though, neither Young nor I were left with a choice. Before getting back into the helicopter to scan the area, Blacksuit decided suddenly, albeit belatedly, it was important to search the nearby stand of pines and alders *first.* And, hearing it, I felt my hopes sink, thinking our cover couldn't withstand the intense ground level scrutiny it was about to receive—which would mean ultimately a face to face fire fight—a game of quick draw against their infinitely superior automatic weapons.

"Just to be sure," Blacksuit said, as he and his companion began to fan out. They entered our rectangular patch of trees at opposite ends, then weaved their respective ways back and forth thru the manzanita and sage towards our centered position—rifles held with both hands in front and at the ready, while Young Hunter and I lay silent and coiled in the bottom of our holes. I could hear them kicking at the brush trying to flush us, as they came ever nearer. But then suddenly, totally unexpectedly, two short bursts of automatic rifle fire whistled thru the meadow and cut them down.

From a stand of trees opposite and across the clearing, it sounded like a Soviet AK47 and, as quickly as that, in a blink of an eye, they were dead, wordless and motionless on the ground.

And it was silent—all silent in the meadow again—with the *caw* of a scolding jay and the more distant drumming of a woodpecker signatures even of normalcy. A normalcy which was counterfeit, as was the silence, too; as there could be no normal and no returning—with feelings ever heightened of danger and fear.

Slowly, very slowly, I turned my head, seeking eye contact thru the branches with Young Hunter, reading there the same bewilderment I was feeling myself, as my mind struggled with the questions of who had done the killing—how many were out there?—and what was *their* motivation?

Whoever it was, if it came to fire power, my light 30/30 brush gun and Young's pistol were no match for a Russian automatic rifle either, I knew that; and about the best thing we could hope for was that our own presence wasn't known.

We stayed silent on our bellies without moving and watched the empty, but for the helicopter, meadow in front of us. And the minutes dragged by—dragged out to a half hour and beyond—and I thought assuredly that was not a good sign, since it seemed logical that whoever had done the shooting would emerge to inspect the bodies and the chopper, if they thought themselves to be alone. Then belatedly, it came to me that, as an alternative to waiting as we were doing, the killer or killers might be stalking us instead.

Then I felt the hair on the back of my neck stand up and, glancing back over my shoulder, was traumatized by the sight of a very small man in camouflage and black face paint, holding a rifle and looking down on our blinds from only a pace or two behind.

As soon as I saw him, too, he brought the rifle—not surprisingly an AK47—up to his shoulder and very calmly aimed down at us.

"I thought you Indians were supposed to be the best," he said in a contemptuous drawl. "Toss your toys out in front of you, then crawl on out this side."

I tossed the 30/30 several yards out into the meadow, as directed; as did Young, also, the pistol. Then we both crawled out and sat in the dirt with hands on our heads—also on command— facing our captor, who'd backed away from us perhaps ten or fifteen paces and who continued to aim his rifle in our direction.

"Now," he said in his nasal twang, "I want to know who the hell you are, and who you're workin' for? And why you went to all the trouble of burying my buddy out there. And I want to know *now*!"

"Buddy?" I blurted, blankly.

"Yeah, my friend, Jeff Hamil. That was Jeff Hamil you buried out there, my partner in Nam." His voice was tight and angry and very dangerous.

He was, as I said, about fifteen steps from us, and he shifted the black heavy weapon, briefly training it on Young Hunter before swinging it back to me.

"I don't have time to be messin' with ya," he said, "so if I were you I'd speak up *now*! Who was it sent you up here to bury him?"

Given the state he was in, what I did next probably wasn't too smart either; but the significance of his earlier statement hit me suddenly, and it was like a light bulb going on in my head. All of a sudden, it registered who he was, and I blurted pretty much out of relief at knowing we were on the same side.

"Is your name Miller?" I said, managing to aggravate him even further by answering his question with a question, and startling him besides.

He hesitated for a moment, then responded thru gritted teeth. "Maybe it is and maybe it ain't," he said, raising the rifle slightly and seeming to tighten his finger on the trigger. "How would you know my name, anyway? I've never seen you before in my life."

"My name's Tony Hamil," I said, "and I came up here to bury my brother."

He stood eyeing me, the rifle still pointed at my chest, and with the disbelief on his blackened face changing to perplexity.

"Well," he said finally, uncertainly, "you don't sound much like an Indian. But, you sure do look like one."

"Well, I can show you the skin on my leg?" I said, starting to bend forward, but then stopped by the renewed sharpness in his command.

"Slow!" he barked. "Real slow."

Beside me, Young Hunter was frozen like a statue and, for some reason, I noticed him then and was aware of his paralyzed fear. Still, I reached for the pants material and pulled it up slowly, as I'd been instructed, revealing the startling whiteness of my calf—a lack of color we jokingly refer to up North as our "Alaskan rust".

He licked his lips, but still kept the rifle trained on my middle.

"So what if your legs are a sickly white," he said, "why is that supposed to make me believe you're Tony Hamil?"

"Well," I said, after slowly lowering the pant's leg back down, "what if I told you all about your being isolated alone with my brother on the Ho Chi Minh Trail and about your springing him from a Russian trap set below a foot bridge crossing over a gorge. He wrote and told me about that after you got him out."

He sighed then and, lowering the weapon, leaned heavily up against a nearby boulder, seeming suddenly even smaller and actually forlorn.

"I should've been up here with him," he said with a certain argumentiveness. "If I'd have been here, they never would have done this to him. Never!" He nodded his head in the direction of the grave.

"Well," I said, trying to ease him, "it wasn't your fight, I guess, and you couldn't be fighting his battles all your life."

But he bristled again. "It *was* my fight though!" he shot back. "It was my fight and your fight and anybody's fight, who cared anything about anything. I knew what he was doin'. I was giving him the explosives to do it, but I was *retired*."

139

He spat the word contemptuously, as if it were dirty in his mouth, and then cursed himself for being what he termed "too yellow to get involved".

Then we were all three silent again, as he returned to slumping against the rock. Young Hunter shifted slightly, though, into an Indian squatting position and, noticing him again, Miller wanted to know more.

"Who's he?" he said. "And what's with the Indian look, anyway?"

"He *is* an Indian," I said, squatting up on my haunches then, also, and beginning to tell our story while he remained still beside the rock. I told him about Joe's letter and Jeff's girl friend and the police and the Hamil's ties to the Indians—an overview at least—and he listened intently, not interrupting and only fidgeting when I reached the part about the girl.

Afterwards, we were again silent while he sat obviously considering—mulling it over—until finally I asked him how he'd come to be there in the mountains at that precise time, too.

He licked his lips nervously again, then suddenly squatted down, also, facing us—a gnome like little man, with receding sandy hair and angular features under the black paint, still with the rifle, crosswise now in front of him.

"You know," he said, slowly clasping and unclasping his hands on stock and fore piece, "I just had this feelin'. It was the day after I read about the boat blowin' up. I knew Jeff'd done it. I brought him the claymores a couple of nights before. But then, there was this empty feeling—just a feelin' of . . . I can't explain it . . . of desolation. His voice trailed away.

"I guess we went thru too much stuff together for too long a time."

Again he was quiet for awhile; then surprised suddenly with his next statement. "I knew the girl, too," he said. "Sue Marie. I met her once when I came up to Reno to see Jeff—before he started blowin' up everything. He was really in love with her, and I thought maybe he was gonna be all right. But then, I remember she started hinting at some liberal anti-war, anti-male stuff—like she was just tryin' it out—and then when Jeff went off to the head, I told her some stuff of my own. Stupid! We were drinkin' beer, but

I should have kept my mouth shut. She just might finger me, too, if they get to askin' her a lot of questions about Jeff. She'll remember me because of what I said, and because Jeff went on about our bein' in Nam together."

He was still squatting in front of us in the dirt, now patting the gun stock absently.

"If they trace me to LA and find out I'm in the armory there," he said, "it won't take a lot of brilliance to figure out where Jeff got his ordnance from."

He shook his head worriedly, obviously picturing something in his mind and then staring blankly—while once again Young Hunter and I waited in silence.

"Well," he said finally, more upbeat, "I've got a couple of offers in Africa. There's always a war going on over there."

Still, I hadn't made the transition yet, and was not so concerned with his side of things. And, I was still curious.

"If you saw us burying Jeff, why didn't you open up on us?" I blurted then, breaking in on his train of thought.

He stared uncomprehendingly for a minute, then seemed to come back from a long way away, asking me to repeat the question.

"Look," he said, when I did, "I've been waiting, watching over in those trees for almost a week, listening to those animals getting at Jeff. And I nearly did shoot you—you don't even want to know how close it was."

He paused, then muttered again seemingly to himself. "When I thought about it, it didn't jibe with the chopper tracks, you bein' Indian, or appearin' to be, and bein' upset like you were."

"You guys might just as well get on the trail and move on, though." He stood up, waving his arm towards the West, as if in dismissal; and for a brief moment, I was tempted to do exactly what he said.

But then—because of his friendship with Jeff and because he'd most probably saved our lives—I followed him instead, as did Young, as he walked out to examine each of the dead bodies. He stood staring down at Blacksuit, the first we came to, for what seemed a full minute, holding the rifle in one hand, while fingering some kind of animal tooth which hung from a short gold chain around his neck. Then, without a word, suddenly kicked dirt in the corpse's twisted face. And repeated the ritual soon afterward with the white suited pilot as well.

Then he walked away quickly out towards the helicopter, then turned suddenly on his heel and came back to us, obviously agitated and, I thought, dangerous.

"I'm gonna put'em back in the chopper," he said, "and set fire to it, so it'll look like a crash."

And it was an idea completely foreign to me—as foreign to me as killing—because all my life, as a Hamil, I'd thought always of nurturing and protecting Nature, and never of burning it. And, I protested.

"We'll wind up burning hundreds of acres of meadow and trees," I said, "before fire crews can even get to it!"

"Don't you understand," he retorted with a kind of controlled fury, his blue eyes seeming electric and piercing into me, and his words armed with an irrefutable logic. "A few hundred acres is nothing compared to our lives, and in fact you're the one most probably would be blamed."

I stood staring at him, a man half my size, and not liking it—not liking what it was costing, and with a beginning knowledge that it might cost a lot more before it was finished. Still, I bowed my head in agreement then because it did seem the only immediate solution. And afterwards, Young and I helped him get the two bleeding bodies up into the chopper's bay and finally into the pilot and co-pilot seats.

Back outside, when we'd gathered up our various gear, he started the burning with an explosive AK47 spraying of the helicopter's fuel tanks. And, with black smoke billowing upwards and flames quickly crackling thru the brush towards the trees, we loped single file across the meadow and on down the trail to the West.

Then, there was a release, and it felt good to be free of that hellish place, even with the fire burning behind us. Young was in the lead, or "on the point" as they say militarily, with me second and Miller in the rear. And we ran for at least a mile, passing a branch trail that headed off from the far side of the meadow to the South; then dropped down thru a broad stand of pines; climbed again thru rocks and manzanita and more pines; then descended again. Until finally, Young Hunter paused in a little clearing by a stream to drink. I pulled up alongside. And Miller was gone.

Chapter Nineteen

We hiked all night—Young Hunter and I—leaving the fire burning above us in the high meadows, winding our way in the darkness back down the steep miles of trail to the Lake. If we could reach Young's truck by dawn, then we would avoid the scrutiny of Forestry Department fly-overs. And of course, it was critical that we not be picked up as suspects in setting the fire.

In the last hour before daylight, we had to abandon caution, too, hurrying on the loose shale and risking sprained or broken ankles. Still, we were fortunate and reached the truck just as the gray dawn was turning to light gold. We approached the truck cautiously, watching from the trees, but there was no one stirring, either near the truck or across the highway at the log house Zephyr Cove Inn.

We loaded our gear quickly, and Young drove us out onto the highway, heading back in the direction of Reno which was about fifty miles distant. And as the sun rose rapidly in the East, it was soon apparent from the smoke and red haze that our fire had burned throughout the night.

Still, we didn't talk much at all, and I think it was because what we'd been thru was so profound that neither of us had really come to grips with it. In my own case, I felt as if I'd lost myself, and it seemed impossible that just a few days earlier I'd been the confident captain of an Alaskan crab boat, transformed now into a nervous woman *of a* man, dressed up in an Indian costume, sucked down inexorably and inevitably by Nevada's whirling cesspool of corruption.

Worrying, I rubbed more Indian dye from a small jar I'd brought on my face and neck and hands, repairing those areas smeared and faded from my sweating. Then on the way down out of the mountains, we encountered two highway patrol cars, both hurrying oppositely, back up towards the Lake—perhaps on account of the fire or related business. And on each sighting, I sucked in my breath involuntarily (as did Young, I think). But in each case, there was no slowing down or registering of any sort; so that afterwards, we were somewhat more relaxed.

Rationally too, I realized that there shouldn't be initial suspicion, at least not until the *crashed* helicopter was discovered, recalling, too, that most human-caused fires occurred there in the summer when hikers and campers were more prevalent.

Still, as we neared the Reno outskirts—scattered service stations and trailer parks on the edge of the sage—anxiety heightened again; and with images of Jeff's body and the killings we'd seen still vivid in mind, I thought grimly that such feelings probably would follow both Young and me to some degree the rest of our lives, however long or short they might be.

Once inside the city limits, and paranoid, we watched for other cars that might be following us, taking several diversionary routes. But then spotting nothing, finally, around ten o'clock, we pulled into the Indian village. Young Hunter parked outside his house, and I was keenly aware of his unease, too, although he'd said little. Afterwards going in to be with his woman, a different man on different ground—leaving me to hide once more in the pump house out behind.

Then the day dragged on interminably and forever, sleepless and with nervousness unbearable. And I tried to divert away from it, forcing myself to think about Alaska, while once again trying to control the fear that I'd never be there again—homesick and comparing things there with the things where I was—everything from plants and animals and climate to people and their philosophies. I thought about my boat and my crew, about the gray days and the wind and waves and handling the heavy gear on deck, and the indescribable exhilaration afterwards—of being safely back in the inlet, having cheated death another time—drinking brandied coffee with the crew around the dim lit table in the cabin and knowing we'd be at the dock in the morning with a good catch to unload. I thought of clear still days on the inlet in summer, with the water a silver mirror; of my wife's brown lithe body and of playing with our son in a field of wildflowers on the hill. I thought of the snow, the crunching sounds of it under my boots on a winter's day, my breath a cloud of steam in the blindingly cold air; and of stalking a great brown bear, which in turn was stalking me. And I remembered knowing humility in the face of God's awesome Nature—of understanding the fragility of the human experience and the extreme tenuousness of our lives there. Knowing that the perception of this reality is somehow dulled in so-called "civilized" society—replaced by a kind of plastic coated lie, that if all the right foods are eaten, and purified, distilled waters are drunk, and the right exercises are indulged in religiously, death *may be* stymied. And just the suggestion that it *might be* is enough to get people to believe subconsciously that it *will be*—hence the softening of that unpleasant terror to the point where people don't get prepared.

In this, there is a dulling of all the senses, too, it seems—i.e., 'if I'm not really going to die, then I have time to look at the pretty flowers later on; or listen to a songbird on some other morning; or, more importantly, not love my children when I feel tired; or not acknowledge another's loving attention as that person's valuable treasure—unless it absolutely suits me at the time.'

In the early evening, the Council appeared again, coming in silently and solemnly along with Young Hunter. And after all were situated, Young related in their language all that had happened in the mountains behind the Lake.

In a seated circle on the floor around us—while Young sat beside me on the cot—they listened with great soberness, black eyes flashing on occasion from Young Hunter to myself, but otherwise remaining impassive until Young had finished.

And in the crowded confines of the underground room, I examined it again myself—as they were doing—wondering if they might not fault me for burying Jeff's body beforehand and thus drawing attention to our presence. And in a way, I wished that Miller hadn't killed the two men, though if he hadn't, it was quite probable Young and I would have had to do so to survive. Still, it very well could spell trouble for all of them, and for that I was genuinely sorry, sitting convicting myself even if they were not.

When Young Hunter finished, there was very little talk, only a muttered phrase or two here and there, followed by a time of silent contemplation. And I sat on the edge of the bed waiting with Young alongside, feeling I was awaiting a jury at deliberation time, solemn and unhurried and patient and wise.

Then finally, it was the old chairman who spoke, leaning forward on the room's single chair which had been ceded to him again because of his rank and age, his white hair contrasting startlingly with his dark, leathery and much wrinkled skin.

"Tony Hamil," he said in his deep tones, "we're all glad Jeff's friend killed those criminals. It was right and just. And it's right that you buried Jeff and took him from the animals when you did."

The others murmured their assent, and I sighed involuntarily and with relief, being not only troubled by the killings at that point but, as I've said, very much worried about the effects upon the lives of these friends.

"What do you think, Tony?" the old chief asked.

And then I wondered immediately if the old man were asking me really if now I didn't think I should leave—having put them in enough jeopardy. Or if perhaps he was asking if, in view of the killings, and of Jeff's murder being avenged, I didn't want to escape quickly, and, for the time forget about Joe.

And, I paused for a moment before answering, gathering myself as they would have done.

"I want to thank you," I spoke softly at length, "and I'm very sorry for bringing this danger to you. You know when I came here it was because of Joe's letter—because of wanting to help Joe and just to find out about Jeff. I had no intention of being involved in killing anyone."

I was hoarse and more keyed up than I knew, and for a moment couldn't go on—until the old chief encouraged me once again.

"It's all right, Tony," he said, "we all here know that sometimes, to happen, things have a soul of their own."

"Look," I said chokingly, "I'm going to help Joe get out of there. That's what I came here to do, and I'm going to do it. But you've all done enough, and I'm going to hide some other place!"

And I stood up amongst their murmuring as if to leave; but immediately, Young Hunter stood in front of the steps with his arms folded.

"No," the old chief said sharply. "Hear us out, Tony. You haven't heard us yet!"

And the command in his great deep voice stopped me in spite of myself. So that afterwards with a sigh, I sat back down.

"Tony," he said, and there was now a resigned sadness in his voice, "Tony, have you forgotten? Already you are on the television—a star. And once they find the helicopter, I think that they will make the connection to you."

I listened and he went on, one side of his leathered face twitching slightly, and his eyes mirroring much pain.

"There's no guarantee the bodies were burned up in the fire, you know," he said, "and they may be able to see that those men were shot."

I waited, while he and the others studied me and the effect his words were having. Then he went on.

"Tony, I have to consider what is best for all of us—for my people. It is my position here.

"Tony, we are small and weak—just surviving. And there are some of us like Joe who are in prison unjustly, or have been killed. But we have had to balance those events with what is right for most of us. We cannot commit suicide as a people because of what's happened to some. Instead, for the rest of us to live at all, we must remain in defense."

Head down now, I waited; and, when he spoke again, it was more slowly, and with his deep voice softened.

"Tony, if you stay and they come looking around—and they will come because after while they'll remember we are connected to your family—then, if some little child in the village blurts out that he's seen you, we'll all pay much more than the anguish we feel now—knowing Joe is where he is.

"Joe is an old man now, Tony; but Young Hunter, your brother here, is not, and he's got a family and may be in trouble already. What if they catch this Miller and he talks to them? They have ways to make even the strongest men talk, you know?

"And you, Tony, what about you? We know that you love Joe and that you were close. But what of your wife and your baby son? They are the ones who need you more. And Tony, we don't expect you to put Joe ahead of them. You don't have to do this to prove to us anything. We know you, Tony Hamil. And your family. And we will never forget."

Chapter Twenty

Then more than ever, I was like them—one of them—a once proud people, beaten down, acquiescing, overpowered and too weak to fight back. Smothered by a blanket of evil, with no ideas of victory anymore. Striving to stay unnoticed as a means of surviving. And with my "uncle," Indian Joe, as their poster child, rejected in an insane world not of his own making.

Oliver Word, the half breed cropduster, banked his little cream colored Cessna sharply to the North after takeoff, and I looked down on the harsh dry land of rock and sagebrush covered hills—Indian land—where for the most part now only the ghosts of the past could dwell, and where Joe would never walk again. And I hated it—not the land, but the Nevada mobster politicians who'd made it thus—who with their police state, Gestapo tactics had driven good men like Joe and my brother to violent acts; who'd spat on the Indian people and destroyed our environmental heritage forever—who, in fact, had turned me into a fugitive.

And flying away, I felt the desolation of deserting, wanting more than ever to stay and fight, feeling now in my bones, I suppose, what my dad, Ned, had always felt. And understanding finally why he hadn't just picked up and moved us all away. Understanding just how wrong it was what they'd done—what they'd gotten away with—and sick to my stomach every time I even thought of Joe.

Oliver Word, who'd learned to fly in the service and who cropdusted lands all the way into Idaho, flew me as a stowaway to Boise and, bucking strong headwinds, North into Canada, avoiding the scattered population centers of Grangeville and Kellogg and Sandpoint, and landing finally on a dirt road outside the town of Creation. I paid him a thousand dollars for the service, though he refused when I said I'd send him more—being himself the nephew of the old chief, and with a breaking heart for Joe as well.

The bulk of the remaining money I'd given to Young Hunter to fix up his house—for the danger I'd placed him in, and his family—with just enough left for a Trailways bus ticket up thru British Columbia to Prince George, and an airplane ticket to the Aleutians after I'd hitchhiked with a trucker into Anchorage.

It was not exactly a triumphant return though and, while Two Waters, my wife, was deeply pleased to see me, she quickly picked up on my sadness and dissatisfaction. Sure, I was relieved to be home with her and our son and, doubtless after a time, would settle back into our old routines. Still, I knew I'd be haunted by it always now, and that things could never really be the same.

"Tony, I think they got Jeff. I had a dream. I think he's dead. Come!"

Joe's words echoed in my soul. And the knowledge that he was there, still wondering, still not knowing still dreaming seemed sometimes more than I could bear.

Afterwards, after I'd had another talk with Prentice, the Englishman at the dock, then the boat logs for all the trips made during my absence were altered to show me as onboard and captain. My crew was apprised and in agreement, as were the Constable and Justice of the Peace, and everyone else who might matter. Because it was still Alaska, after all. And with that, I knew there'd be no extraditing of me from there—not ever.

If the gangster enemies of the Hamil's should ever come to the Aleutians to take revenge on the Bear, or upon Two Waters, or Joseph, their baby son, maybe they'd succeed. But then again, by the grace of the good Lord Jesus, maybe they would not. Every day we live with that; but every day we live.

THE END

Printed in the United States
126776LV00010B/99/P

9 781600 472305